Media Training A-Z

Testimonials for
Media Training Worldwide

"TJ Walker is the leading media trainer in the world and Media Training A-Z is the ideal resource for presenting well on TV. I'd highly recommend this book for anyone who is planning on doing any TV work."

– Stu Miller
Viacom News Producer

"I put the skills learned to excellent use. I was told by the producer that it was refreshing to work with someone who was comfortable in front of the camera and could get their message points out. So, kudos to you for training me! It was a wonderful experience."

– Roxanne Moster
UCLA

"Media Training Worldwide is flat out better than any other presentation training firm we have ever used. They get better results in one day of training than other companies do in two day seminars. The bottom line is that Media Training Worldwide changes our executives for the better; when they leave a Media Training Worldwide workshop they speak with much more confidence and passion. TJ Walker has made radical and permanent positive transformations with many of our employees. I can't imagine using any other training firm."

– Jim Miller
Amerada HESS

"Anyone suffering from MDS (Media Deficiency Syndrome) will find this book an immediate antidote and long term, if taken regularly, a cure."

– John F. Budd
The Omega Group

"Over the years I've been a fan of TJ Walker and his rigorous approach to media training. If TJ had his way, no client would ever lose a media interview. And, if every executive would take the time to read this latest edition, he or she probably never will. TJ is clearly a veteran of the broadcast and print interview world and his tips are well worth reading. I know I've learned some new strategies."

– Edward Aloysius Moed
Peppercom, Inc.

"As a crisis communications consultant, I think I know a great deal about media training. However I learned a LOT by reading TJ Walker's book – Especially when it comes to tips and techniques for presenting yourself in as positive a way as possible during TV interviews. TJ is truly an expert in this arena and his advice is valuable and practical. His writing style is conversational – enjoyable to read and easy to digest. I highly recommend this book to my clients."

– Judy Hoffman
Principle JCH Enterprises and author of
"Keeping Cool on the Hot Seat"

"A handy crash course for the busy or new executive encountering the media for the first time."

— Michael J. London
Michael J. London & Associates

"I've read a variety of media training books over the years and never found the exact type of training manual with content that I could just hand to a client for their review. That's until I read TJ's media training book. It incorporates most of the media techniques and approaches that I have emphasized with my clients over the years -- and goes well beyond that -- to help the novice and seasoned business professional alike with interview and media training tips. It really allows the most senior on-camera client to still learn about news interview techniques without insulting them or making them feel like their presentation is faulty or embarrassing. TJ's approach is well-organized and definitely concise so you can easily learn effective interview techniques".

— Ron Dresner
President
Your PR Department, LLC

"This comprehensive guide is a 'must-have' for every communicator and pr practitioner. It's an invaluable resource and the ideal tool following professional training."

— Nancy Friedman
Nancy J. Friedman Public Relations

"As the CEO of the fastest growing independent PR firm in the U.S., we realize that clients, corporations and executives need to understand how to be best prepared to speak with the media in order to communicate clear messages, and utilize every second on TV and every inch of ink. TJ Walker's book clearly communicates the necessary tools to ensure that image and messages are captured. From the color and design of one's shirt, to hand motions, style of answers to repeating messages over and over, media training can better prepare any and all for their PR Needs."

— Ronn D. Torossian
5W Public Relations

"TJ Walker was able to help my entire team operate more efficiently [and] maximize their message penetration to their audience. I can tell you his pace was incredible, he was extremely articulate and he got the whole group involved. We really enjoyed the day."

— Michael Gallant
EMC

"Media Training A-Z is a concise, highly readable, user-friendly book--written by one who has been practicing what he preaches--that should be in the briefcase of anyone who dares to speak to the public."

— George Haber
Information Services

This Book Is Dedicated To
Great And Aspiring Speakers Everywhere.
~ TJ Walker

Receive FREE VIDEOS!

To receive weekly video tips focusing on speaking to the media send a blank email to:

freemediavideo@mediatrainingworldwide.com

Published by **Media Training Worldwide**

Media Training Worldwide provides more media and presentation training workshops and seminars than any other company in the world. We also publish more than 100 media and presentation training books, DVDs, CDs, and other information products and are the premier presentation/media training publisher in the world.

www.mediatrainingworldwide.com

Library of Congress Catalog Card Number: 2004115412
ISBN: 1-932642-36-6

Printed in the United States of America
Sixth Edition: January 2011

First Edition: December 2004
Developmental Editor: Deborah Knox
Copy Editor: Joni Mitchell
Book Design: Kristopher Gentile

Media Training A-Z

A Complete Guide To Controlling Your
Image, Message, & Sound Bites

By TJ Walker

MEDIA
TRAINING
WORLDWIDE

Table of Contents

Introduction

All of my media training clients want the same things when it comes to dealing with the media. First, when facing an audience, they would like to come across as comfortable, confident and relaxed (and they'd actually like to feel comfortable, confident and relaxed, too). Next, they'd like to be able to come up with and deliver a clear-cut, simple message; answer questions in a thoughtful manner; and ensure that the exact quotes, or sound bites, they want get into the story. (A sound bite is a bite out of the sounds you are making with your words during an interview that actually ends up on a TV or radio newscasts) I use the term sound bite and quote interchangeably throughout this book. This book is a compilation of insights I've gleaned over the last 20 years of trying to help clients accomplish these goals.

The Enemy Within

It never ceases to amaze me how creative and resourceful people can be when trying to control the outcomes of media interviews. The following is a partial list of tactics used by would-be media manipulators.

- demanding to know all the questions that will be asked in advance
- setting restrictions on what topics can be addressed
- stating what questions must be avoided
- requesting that all questions be faxed in advance
- insisting that the written story be sent to them for final approval before publishing

- demanding the right to fax in their answers rather than having a face-to-face or phone interview
- requesting that a friendly or sympathetic reporter be assigned to their story
- setting a strict time limit on the interview, e.g., 15 minutes (and not because the interviewee has a plane to catch or any other urgent business)
- asking for the right to videotape or audiotape the interview

This is only a partial list of extreme and counterproductive measures that people take to "control" the interview. In my professional opinion, all of these tactics are a complete and utter waste of time, and they can only have a negative impact on the story and your long-term reputation. (The only exception: if you are a $20-million-per-film movie star, you can get away with making demands such as these.)

All of these tactics are an attempt to control the reporter. Unfortunately, the reporter is the one part of the process over which you, as the interview subject, have no control. For many people whose careers involve communication through the media, this realization is an important psychological breakthrough.

YOU HAVE ZERO CONTROL OVER REPORTERS, SO GET OVER IT.

What can you control?

YOU HAVE 100 PERCENT CONTROL OVER WHAT COMES OUT OF YOUR MOUTH.

For starters, you can come up with a clear, simple, easy-to understand, interesting message. Next, you can package your message in media-friendly sound bites. Finally, you can talk to reporters in a comfortable, confident way that makes you look your best. These are the three elements over which you, the interviewee, have total control. 100 percent control.

How effective would Bill Gates of Microsoft be if he spent 100 percent, or even 80 percent, of his time trying to figure out what Larry Ellison of Oracle was going to do next week? Sure, Gates might be interested. He might appreciate market intelligence from time to time. But Gates has to spend most of his time worrying about what Microsoft employees are actually doing next week. Why? Because that's what he has the most control over.

The real problem most of these would-be media manipulators have is that they don't realize that they already have tremendous power to control every interview. That power derives from the fact that they have 100 percent control over what comes out of their own mouth. Never forget this: the reporter has 100 percent control over the questions and the topics, but we interviewees have 100 percent control over our answers.

When clients complain to me about a so-called bad journalist who "burned" them in the past and who is "out to get them," I always ask for proof. The clients then might mention a previous article that made them look bad that included damaging quotes.

I ask, "But did you say this quote?"

Invariably, the clients say, "They used a totally negative quote that they knew would make me look bad."

Again, I ask, "But is that an accurate quote?"

They respond, "The quote was totally taken out of context."

Then I remind them that every quote in every newspaper, radio or TV report is taken out of context. Any one sentence you say is taken out of the context of a 10- or 20-minute conversation. Since you know this will happen before you even start the interview, it's rather pointless to complain after the fact that your comments were "taken out of context."

Finally, I ask one more time, "Were you quoted accurately?'

A look of frustration comes over them and then they confess, "Yes! It was an accurate quote."

And I respond, "So what you are really complaining about is that the reporter listened to you, accurately wrote down what you said, accurately quoted you, but now, since you don't like the quote and you feel it makes you look bad, you want to blame someone else for your own mistakes. You'd like to blame the reporter for not trying to make you look good, is that correct?"

At this point the clients are speechless because they know that this is exactly the situation, and they suddenly realize how foolish they have been.

I'm not saying reporters don't make mistakes – they do. I'm not implying there aren't unethical reporters who occasionally just make stuff up (the New York Times and USA Today have had their share of such reporters). But I've found it extraordinarily rare for people to be upset about quotes and statements attributed to them that were fabricated. What angers people most is when their own words are used against them to make them look foolish. Remember, it's not the reporter's job to make you look good; that's your job. If you go into an interview without a clear message and well-thought-out sound bites, you just might have an enemy ready to destroy your career. But if you want to locate this enemy, don't stare down the reporter across the table. Instead, look in the mirror.

The One Common Leadership Trait
Why Communication Skills Matter

Political, business and cultural leaders come in many sizes, shapes and styles, displaying varying degrees of skill. Some rise at 4 a.m.; some work from noon to 2 a.m. Some are teetotalers; some like to drink a fifth a day.

Leaders often become leaders because they are experts at motivating other people to do that which they would normally not want to do. Leaders learn how to delegate effectively. Corporate leaders can delegate sales, advertising and accounting tasks. Political leaders can delegate the planning and fighting of wars.

However, there is one thing that all real leaders know they cannot delegate: speaking on behalf of their organization to the outside world. A President must be able to speak on behalf of the entire American public when addressing the country and the rest of the world. A corporate CEO must be able to speak on behalf of the company to clients, customers, employees, vendors, analysts, investors and the news media. This cannot be delegated to staff.

That is why the one most common trait shared by true leaders is the ability to communicate well, especially through the spoken word. Of course, speaking styles vary among leaders, but at some point most leaders find a way to be effective when they are speaking.

There is more to being a leader than just speaking well. Having wisdom, good judgment and solid principles are also essential. But try to imagine a wise and principled Winston Churchill who was afraid to give a speech. Impossible! Churchill's wisdom, judgment and principles would never have been brought to the world stage if he had not been able to communicate them effectively via the spoken word.

More than height or looks or wealth or even charm, mastering public speaking is the one true X-factor that determines a great leader. In fact, having strong communication skills can sometimes override the fact that there is nothing else a leader can do in a certain situation. Take, for example, the case of New York City Mayor Rudy Giuliani during the 9/11 crisis. By every traditional measure of leadership (e.g., making unpopular decisions, encouraging the public to make sacrifices, anticipating and preventing future dangers), how did Giuliani fare?

I would contend that Giuliani didn't take any of the actions most commonly associated with great acts of political leadership that we may associate with Lincoln or Churchill. (I'm not criticizing Giuliani; I don't think the mayor of any city would have been able to do much more than Giuliani did. Disclosure: I even voted for Giuliani in his reelection bid.) But why, in the aftermath of 9/11, was Giuliani hailed as a hero across the country and around the world? What did Giuliani actually DO to achieve such universal acclaim?

He talked. He communicated. He expressed emotions. He talked, without notes, from the head and the heart. For several weeks, Giuliani was the nation's talk-show-host-in-chief. A la Oprah, Giuliani was also a ratings hit, especially since he was a more talented communicator than the New York governor or even the president of the United States at the time.

The public so deeply believes that outstanding communication skills are a hallmark of a great leader that sometimes delivering a knockout single speech or series of public presentations is enough to etch an image of heroic leadership in the public's mind.

You Can Get A Second Chance To Make A Great Impression

Of course, you never want to go into a presentation opportunity thinking, "OK, I'll be lousy here because I can always do better next time." That's highly counterproductive. However, one bad speech, or even a string of poor presentations, will not kill you as long as you hone your skills and start to deliver great talks. Your peers and colleagues in your company and industry will start to think of you as a great communicator in a short period of time if you start giving excellent presentations, no matter how many lackluster speeches you've given in the past.

By all accounts, then-Governor Bill Clinton flubbed his keynote address at the 1988 Democratic Convention in Atlanta. He went way too long and lost his audience, and he was roundly booed. The only time he elicited a cheer was when he said, "And in conclusion . . ." That brought down the house –

not exactly what a speaker is hoping for. Clinton didn't wait long to rehabilitate his image. He went on the Today Show the very next morning to make fun of himself and to reposition himself as a more engaging speaker. Over time, and many well-delivered speeches later, even Clinton's worst enemies (He did have a few, didn't he?) forgot the debacle of '88.

If you ask Americans who were some of the greatest speakers of the 20th century, President John F. Kennedy makes the top ten on any list, but he was not always considered a good communicator. As late as the mid-'50s, when Kennedy was a senator, he was known as a lackluster speaker who came across as shy, awkward, unenergetic and not very interesting. I've had Democratic activists who heard Kennedy speak to small political clubs in New York City tell me, "Kennedy came across like any other run-of-the-mill city council candidate – he was mediocre at best."

Jack Valenti, former aide to Lyndon Johnson, has written that the first time he saw Kennedy speak in the '50s, the then-senator read with his head buried in notes – only his thick hair was visible to the audience. Valenti even noted that as president, Kennedy's hands shook from nervousness while speaking.

But Kennedy changed. He practiced. He improved.

You can, too.

Chapter 1:
Warming Up

Don't Think On Your Feet – Think At Your Seat

My clients often tell me before we begin a training session that they want to learn how to "think on their feet" better during presentations, question and answer sessions, and media interviews.

My response is, "Why?"

Being able to think on one's feet is highly overrated. It is far better to develop the discipline of preparing in advance and rehearsing. Of course, this is hard work, but if you consistently think about your message and all of the issues surrounding your topic, you will rarely be surprised.

So if you want to appear to be good at thinking on your feet, spend some time thinking at your seat in front of your computer, writing down notes, outlines, bullet points, and sample questions and answers. Then you can make it all look easy.

In The Moment

To truly excel as a communicator in the media or in front of an audience, you must project that you are "in the moment." That means you have to be so comfortable with what you are speaking about and how you are speaking that nothing can bother you, and you can react and change course in less than a second.

Nervous speakers are sometimes so focused on their prepared speeches that they wouldn't notice it if half of their audience fell over from heart attacks. An in-the-moment speaker is constantly tracking the eyes and body language of individual audience members. If you are truly in the moment, you can alter, adjust, fine-tune, stop, speedup or slowdown instantly because you are reading your audience. That means you are so comfortable that you can instantly toss out an idea that comes to mind or respond to an audience member's reaction on the spot. An in-the-moment media communicator is never thrown for a loop by a reporter, host or caller, because he or she is focused 100 percent on the question of the moment, not preoccupied by what to say in 5 or 10 seconds.

All great communicators use a conversational tone when speaking to their audiences, and nothing simulates the look and feel of an actual conversation more than being in the moment. It doesn't matter if the person listening to you is your spouse at the breakfast table or 10,000 people in a convention hall.

It takes more than a few moments to become in the moment. Don't expect to operate from this disposition in your first, or even tenth, major speech or media appearance. It takes time and persistence, but it is well worth the effort for you and your audiences.

Got No Time

People tell me all the time, "TJ, I'm much too busy to prepare for my media interviews by writing down message points and creating sound bites in advance." Hey, we all have busy lives; I can respect that. There is only one small problem: these people always spend more time dealing with the media ultimately than people who prepare properly do.

Here's the typical scenario: Mr.-I'm-too-busy-to-prepare gets a phone call from a reporter. He drops everything and says, "I'd be happy to talk to you right now," and then conducts the interview for the next hour.

I ask, "How did the interview go?'

And he responds, "Great, the reporter talked to me for a whole hour!"
At this point, unless this is a paying client, I restrain myself from saying, "That's awful! That means it took you an hour before you said anything interesting."

One of the biggest misconceptions in the media business is that the longer a reporter talks to you, the better the interview went. Quite often a reporter will talk to you for a long time because it takes you forever to say anything interesting enough to use as a possible quote.

If you talk to some of the most widely quoted experts on the planet (e.g., Norm Ornstein, Alan Dershowitz), they will tell you that many of their interviews last less than a couple of minutes. When calling these pros, reporters know that they will get juicy sound bites without wasting anybody's time.

How you use your time with the media is critical. The people who dive right into interviews without preparing do so because they think that they are too busy to prepare and believe they are saving time this way. That makes about as much sense as building a house without a blueprint.

Look at how the amateur media "expert" and the media pro use their time.

The amateur media expert spends one hour on the phone with the reporter, getting zero sound bites on their message and maybe one sound bite off-message.

Total time spent: one hour.

The media pro asks the reporter what the interview topic is and when the deadline is. He tells the reporter that now is not a convenient time to talk and that he will call back before the deadline. Next, he spends 10 minutes brainstorming for message points and narrowing them down to no more than three. After that, he spends five minutes crafting sound bites. Next, he calls the reporter and conducts a five-minute interview chock-full o' sound bites. Finally, the media pro spends 30 seconds the next day clipping out the news article, which contains three or more of his preplanned quotes.

Total time spent: 20 minutes 30 seconds.

So you tell me, who is saving time?

Consistency Isn't So Foolish

The biggest problem facing most of my speech and media training clients is that they change the way they talk once the video camera is on them or once they stand up to practice a speech. When most people come into my office and sit down, they are relaxed. They communicate expressively with hand gestures, body motion, facial expressions and a conversational tone of voice. So far, so good. But the second I say, "Let's now do a practice interview or speech, and we will record it," a transformation occurs. It's like when Dr. David Banner turns into the Incredible Hulk, only in reverse. Business executives who were engaging, confident, vocal and alive shrink before my eyes. Their speaking volume decreases. Their voices flatten out. Their hands stop moving. Their bodies become stiff. Their heads become frozen. Getting very sleepy . . .

What's happening here?

When people get nervous, they change their normal presentation style, usually by stiffening up. When it comes to trying to give a good impression to viewers, the results can be disastrous.

The other reason why people change how they talk during speeches or media interviews is the mistaken belief that a so-called "formal" presentation requires a more "formal" style of speaking. This is rubbish. Audiences don't care if you are "formal." They only care about whether you are interesting or boring. Amateur speakers often try to reinvent themselves on the podium or in front of a TV camera. The results are usually less than satisfactory.

Great speakers, however, change very little in their speaking style, regardless of venue or audience size. Bill Clinton speaks the same way, whether it is to one person, 10,000 in a room or 10 million on TV. He is conversational, natural and relaxed in each speaking situation. When Ronald Reagan was in his prime, he was exactly the same way.

So much of my challenge with my speaking and media clients is getting them to stop changing their normal speaking style once they are standing in front of a camera. People erroneously think that a media coach teaches clients to "act" in a more "theatrical" manner – not so.

This is one reason why it is relatively easy for most people to become dramatically better speakers and media communicators in a short period of time. For the most part, it does not require learning a tremendous amount of difficult, new skills. Rather, it is about taking what you already do well in one arena and applying it in another. This is why you can be trained to handle the media in one day, but you can't learn how to play the guitar well in the same amount of time.

Of course, there are some subtle changes that need to be made by speakers depending on the venue. If you are in a large room with 1,000 people in the audience, you need to speak more slowly than usual, using slightly longer pauses. This is because it physically takes longer for your voice to travel around the room. Plus, your gestures need to be slightly bigger than usual to be seen from far away. But other than those minor changes, you should stick with a conversational tone and continue to move naturally.

A common complaint among speakers is that they feel that they are being too repetitive or too consistent. When it comes to communicating well to audiences and the media, there is nothing foolish about consistency, as long as you are consistently conversational and fluid. This is true whether you want to be president or just a more persuasive hobgoblin.

See Yourself On TV
Before You Go On Camera

Media Training Worldwide's New York studio offers an array of simulated environments; from a Satellite Interview, to a mock TV Talk Show setting. You can get comfortable speaking in any situation. To learn more go to:

www.mediatrainingworldwide.com

Chapter 2:
Talking Tips

I Hate My Voice!

At least once a week one of my trainees tells me, "I hate my voice." This is usually followed by a solemn declaration that somehow all recording devices distort his or her voice in an unflattering matter. What's going on here?

Perhaps you have noticed when you hear your own voice on a voicemail or on a home video recording that it doesn't sound like you at all. Actually, it does sound like you, just not the you to whom you are accustomed to listening.

All of us hear our own voice in a distorted manner, only it's not because we have big or small egos. We hear a distorted voice because the bones in our head affect the sound we hear internally. Not only do we hear our voice from the outside, but we also hear it through our skull, which muffles the sound to some extent.

When I play back video recordings of my clients during my trainings, they often react with, "That's not how I really sound." But they notice that when their colleagues are videotaped, what they hear in the recording is exactly what the colleague sounds like live. They then realize that there is nothing wrong with the recording device.

When people tell me they hate their voice, they aren't lying. The real problem for most people, however, is that they are just unfamiliar with their "true" voice, and when they hear their voices for the first time as others do, the difference in perception is so great that it is shocking. It is this disconnect that they don't like, not the actual quality of their voice.

Very few people have voices so mellifluous that they can make a million dollars a year doing voiceovers for TV commercials. The good news is that you don't have to have a voice like that to be an excellent communicator. Barbara Walters has a speech impediment, but she makes more than $18 million a year, in part, with her voice. Rudy Giuliani has a lisp, yet he is paid more than $100,000 for an hour's worth of work giving a speech. John McCain has a sibilant "s" problem, yet he is a political and media darling.

If you think your voice is holding you back, chances are, you are just obsessing over a nonexistent or minor problem.

GET OVER IT!

Protect Your Voice

Your voice is your precious speaking instrument. You must preserve and protect it at all times. Observe these pointers to conserve the strength and quality of your voice before a major speech or presentation:

- Don't sing in the car while listening to the radio. This strains your voice.
- Don't talk at all, except when necessary.
- Don't smoke.

- Don't allow yourself to be around second-hand smoke (stay out of smoky bars in your hotel).
- Don't ever scream!
- If you are swimming, be careful not to exhale through your mouth, as this will strain your vocal chords. Instead, exhale through your nose.

The voice box is a fragile instrument. If you are nice to it, your voice will serve you well. If you abuse your voice, it will abandon you when you need it the most.

You Are What You Drink

Although you should drink plenty of water before you go on TV, heed this advice: "Too much of a good thing isn't a good thing."

I once quickly drank a 32-ounce Big Gulp Coke before a four-hour, talk-radio hosting gig. All of the sudden I got the hiccups. And I don't mean a small case of barely noticeable hiccups. These were violent, chest-cavity spasms that practically knocked me out of my chair every 20 seconds.

To make matters worse, I had no guests for the final two hours of the program and darn few callers. So bathroom breaks were few! Still worse, the hiccups were so ridiculous that I couldn't stop laughing after each episode. Never a good combination – laughter and a full bladder. Fortunately for me, this did not take place during a ratings-sweep week. Don't let this happen to you.

A note on carbonated beverages in general. When you are speaking, you are using your vocal cords. It is your job to protect them, nurture them and make them feel comfortable before you speak so that they won't fail you when you need them. (Although unrelated to protecting your voice, carbonated beverages can also make you hiccup and belch – never attractive in any human encounter – and when consumed in excess, they make you have to use the bathroom.)

Drinking coffee may seem like a good idea, especially before speaking at a breakfast meeting or an early morning talk-radio show. But the caffeine can make you jittery and even more nervous. Starbucks will hate me for this, but even the decafs can be problematic if you put milk in your drink. Milk creates extra mucus in the mouth, which makes it harder to talk clearly. You could also burn your tongue or another body part easily, which would really make for an unpleasant interview. So skip the coffee and avoid milk or anything with milk in it.

Alcohol?

You've got to be kidding. I know many people who claim to have done a shot or two to calm their nerves, especially before speaking at an evening meeting. And yes, some singers use beer to "loosen" their vocal cords, but this is a bad idea for several reasons:

- Alcohol affects the memory, so you are more likely to have your mind go blank in the middle of a speech.
- Alcohol is more likely to make you sweat, which doesn't make a good impression on your audience.

- After you speak, some audience members may come up to say hello or ask questions. If they smell alcohol on your breath, they will not assume that you just had one or two drinks to calm your nerves. Instead, they will assume you are Otis, the Mayberry town drunk from "The Andy Griffith Show."

By now you may be thinking that I want you to die of dry mouth. Not at all. In fact, it is important for you to drink more liquid than usual before speaking and sometimes while you are speaking. The real question is not whether to drink but WHAT to drink.

We have already scratched near-boiling drinks. Ice water is on the other extreme. Unfortunately, too much coldness can tense up your vocal cords. Think of them like a rubber band. They are less flexible when frozen than when warm. So the very best thing for your voice is room-temperature water. If you are speaking for more than 10 minutes or you are a guest on a talk-radio or TV show for more than one 10-minute segment, have a glass of room temperature water by your side at all times.

Your vocal cords will thank you.

Talk To Your Best Friend

Of course, you need to sound intelligent and have your facts straight when talking to the media, but when it comes to being interviewed for TV and radio, you need much more. You need to be able to sound as if you are having a friendly conversation with your best friend in the whole world. You need to be conversational.

- That means DON'T sound as though you are reading or go through some prepared list.
- Listen to the journalist as well as the callers (if it is a talk radio or TV program) and then respond to them in a genuine manner.
- Sound like you are talking to one person, rather than lecturing to a room full of 300 students.
- Avoid big words, insider jargon or fancy acronyms.

If you can sound conversational, many other inadequacies you may have will be forgiven by TV and radio producers and audiences alike. If you don't sound conversational, it won't matter how many facts or insights you rattle off your tongue; you most likely won't be invited back on the air!

Battling The Talk-Radio Clock

So you've been booked as a guest for an entire hour of a talk-radio show to promote your latest book/campaign/new product launch. Finally, you can get away from the tyranny of the sound bite. You will have the luxury of going into great detail and depth. You've got a whole hour, for goodness' sake!

Sorry, but this is not the case. Let's break the hour down minute by minute. From the top of the hour until seven minutes after, you often have news, weather, sports, traffic and some ads to pay the bills. Next, you have ad breaks every seven minutes or so. At the bottom of the hour you may have a short news break, followed by more commercials. And then you may end a minute or two before the top of the hour. So your hour has shrunk to about 39 minutes. But wait, you don't get to talk the whole time – the host is going to want half that time to ask questions and pontificate, so now you are down to approximately 20 minutes.

Wait, we forgot about the callers who want to ask questions – now you are down to about 12 minutes of actual talk time. But still, 12 minutes is a good length of time, right? Especially when you compare it to a three-minute quickie on TV's Good Morning America.

Alas, there is another complication. Research shows that the average talk-radio-program listener tunes in for only 15 minutes. The audience for most talk-radio shows turns over four times during the course of an hour interview. Look at your own experience. If you are driving for 15 minutes from the grocery store to your home, what happens when you get home? Do you sit in your car for another 15 minutes while your ice cream melts just to listen to an expert on the radio? Of course not. You turn both the car and the radio off – that's it.

So if you are a guest on a talk-radio show for one hour, you must remember that you only get about 12 minutes of talk time.

But . . .

You must spread those 12 minutes of talk time over four separate audiences, which means most people listening to you will only hear you for three minutes (12 divided by 4). Therefore, you do not have the luxury of waiting until the end of the show to mention your web site, your campaign, your new product, your toll-free number or your book. You must do these things at least once during every 15-minute sector of the clock, or once ever three minutes in your conversation.

This does not mean that you should mention the name of your book and your publisher in every single sentence. This is annoying and it will alienate you from your audience as well as the talk radio host. But most guests on talk radio go too far in the other direction; they passively wait until the end of the program for the host to plug their reason for appearing on the show. By that time, you've already said goodbye to 75 percent of your audience without ever telling them what you are promoting.

So beware of the hour-long talk-radio interview format – make every minute count.

Do You Use PowerPoint?

8 Quick Tips to help improve your next Presentation:

1. Only One Idea Per Slide
2. Explain Your Point, Then Show The Slide
3. Speaker is the Star, Not The Slides
4. Never Read From Your Slides
5. Use Photos And Drawings
6. Face Your Audience, Not The Slides
7. Avoid Complexity
8. Rehearse, Rehearse, Rehearse

Media Training Worldwide not only helps clients improve their media experiences, but also offers training in Public Speaking and Presenting.

For More Information Contact:
info@mediatrainingworldwide.com

Chapter 3:
Looking "Mahvelous" On TV

TV is a visual medium. It doesn't matter how good your message is or how adroitly you answer questions, if anything about the way you look distracts your audience, your message will not get through. Instead, your audience will fixate on your ugly tie or your fearful expression. So before you even worry about what to say for your next TV interview, prepare for every aspect of your visual presentation.

Do Clothes Make The Man Or Woman?

Many of my speech and media training clients wrongly believe that media/presentation coaches want to focus strictly on style, while the clients consider themselves as purists, focusing only on substance. There is no need to make this distinction. Those who wish to maximize the impact of their substance will spend a great deal of time, money and effort on style as well. The two are as intertwined as strands of a thick rope.

George Washington was quite particular about his white hosiery – he always had a regal look even though he turned down being named king of America. When approaching a city, he would get out of his coach and ride in on white horseback. His image was crucial to his mission.

Winston Churchill gave much attention to the wide wale of his pinstripe, the bigness of his glasses and the use of his cigar. Yes, he had substance, but he always extended it with style.

Do you ever remember seeing a single hair out of place on Margaret Thatcher's head? Of course not. That would have sullied her resolute, strong, principled, political image.

Ronald Reagan would often joke about his age, but he knew that this would work only if he appeared to be vital and healthy. Throughout his eight years in the White House, he never missed a secret Tuesday morning session with his hairdresser, who magically preserved Reagan's hair in the color of chocolate ice cream.

If you want to be effective, your style must complement and extend your message. One reason left-wing, best-selling writer and moviemaker Michael Moore is successful is that his image is totally consistent with his message. He always wears a baseball cap and an old T-shirts and jeans, and he always has exactly 3.5 days of stubble on his face. To convey his "everyman" message, Moore has fashioned the perfect "style." To give him a haircut, close shave and an Armani suit would rob him of his power just as surely as cutting Sampson's hair.

The key is to figure out your own substance/message and then come up with a style that communicates that message. Style is the best marketer substance ever had, and powerful leaders know this and embrace it – they don't whine and show disdain for mundane acts of image building.

To Button Or Not To Button, That Is The Question

Should a man button his suit jacket when appearing on TV? If you look at Regis Philbin, David Letterman or Matt Lauer, the answer is NO. And yet most news anchors and other experts on TV do keep their jackets buttoned.

So which way is better?

As a general rule of thumb for TV appearances, I suggest following what the masters do. If it works for Regis, Dave and Matt, then do it. There is a nice, casual, friendly look to having your jacket unbuttoned and your tie out in the open.

However, in this case, I think it is bad advice for most men and here's why: Regis, Dave and Matt all make millions or tens of millions of dollars a year and can afford personal trainers, personal chefs, tailors, stylists and other groomers who make sure they look perfect in front of the camera every single day. Also, an alteration can be made on the spot if anything isn't hanging just right.

Having your jacket open and your tie exposed works best when you have no form or fit flaws. The problem is that the vast majority of men who are not Regis, Dave or Matt, have some form or fit problems. If you have an extra inch or two around your waist, it will be exposed with an open jacket but concealed with a buttoned coat (provided you haven't put on so much weight that it is straining the buttons on your jacket).

Keeping a jacket buttoned can also help cover up any problems you may be having with your tie. If your tie is too short, your buttoned jacket can conceal the problem; if your tie is too long, you can tuck it into your pants and your buttoned jacket will conceal this, too. If your tie has a tendency to float to the left or the right, a buttoned jacket will help center and anchor it.

Finally, having your jacket buttoned will conceal more of your light-colored shirt while showing more of your dark jacket. This helps direct the viewers' attention to your face (because there is less light fabric attracting attention away from your face), which is exactly where you want it. When viewers look at your face, it is more likely that they will focus on and remember your message.

So when in doubt, button your coat.

Be Cool, Man

TV is a cool medium – we've all heard that before, right? But what does that mean? Most people think it means that you need to act cool, as in low-key, when you are being interviewed on TV. Unfortunately, this leads to disaster.

TV is a cool medium because it cools you down. Someone who speaks with normal energy in a one-on-one conversation can end up looking and sounding flat, boring and monotone on TV. For most people, a TV camera will suck the energy and life out of you. The results? You look and sound dull, unconfident and unconvincing.

There are a couple of factors at play here. For starters, most people are nervous when they go on TV, so they tense up their vocal cords, which lowers their volume and flattens their pitch. Next, some of your natural energy is lost by the time your image goes into a camera, down a bunch of wires, up to a satellite, around the globe, back down to a dish, down more wires and into a TV in someone's living room.

TV is also a cool medium in the sense that old-style preachers and political leaders who are used to yelling in front of large audiences and making grand, sweeping gestures seem too "hot" for TV. While a sweaty face in front of a crowd of 5,000 isn't noticeable, a close-up of one on TV looks disgusting.

However, the reality is that for every person who comes across as too loud or energetic on TV, there are 100,000 people who come across as too soft, weak and unenergetic. In fact, in working with clients for 20 years, I have never yet encountered someone who was too "hot" for TV. However, every week I have clients come in for media training who suffer from energy so low that they look and sound as though they are sleepwalking through their interviews.

Here's what I do:

"Jim, just this one time I want you to indulge me. During this next interview, I want you to go way over the top. I want you to answer your questions and deliver your message as if you were Crazy Eddie screaming at people to buy stereos on a TV commercial. I want you to pretend you are a late-night infomercial guru who is selling snake oil or a get-rich- quick scheme. I promise you, we will never show the tape to anyone – it will just be for fun. Will you do it?"

"OK," says Jim reluctantly.

Now we do a videotaped simulated TV interview with Jim really pouring it on. We finish the interview and I ask Jim, "How did that feel? Wild and crazy? Obnoxious?"

Jim responds, "Yes, that felt ridiculous. I am afraid to even watch it. I'm surprised your neighbors didn't knock on the door to complain about the noise."

Then we go to the videotape (actually the DVD). Jim's eyes start to bug out. He stares in disbelief. What does he see? A normal person who appears to be comfortable, conversational and relaxed.

I ask, "How did it feel when you were doing this?"

Jim said, "It felt horrible, like I was screaming."

"And how does it look now?"

"It looks great. I love the way I'm coming across. I seem totally comfortable and engaged."

"So from now on, you're going to think Crazy Eddie, right?"

"Absolutely . . . that will be cool."

Make Up Your Mind About Makeup

Why do you need to wear makeup when you go on TV? You aren't trying to look like a Hollywood Hunk or Glamour Queen, right?

Unfortunately, you need makeup just to look like you. The bright lights in the studio and on top of the camera will distort your features. What looks like a close shave in person will look like a five o'clock shadow on TV, even if it's only 9 a.m. Clear, normal skin will look splotchy, waxy and plastic on TV. Dark circles under the eyes become more prominent, freckles and shaving nicks that are barely noticeable in person also become much more apparent on TV. Again, with a little makeup, these imperfections fade away.

The heat of the TV lights will also make you sweat, even if you don't normally perspire. Without makeup, your face will look shiny and oily – not very flattering. You may also perspire more because you are nervous. The answer, again, is makeup.

You need to wear makeup not to change your looks, but to keep yourself from having your looks altered beyond recognition. The good news is that you don't have to hire an elaborate, expensive team of makeup artists. All you really need is some basic powder makeup for your face. There is no magic brand or style you need; just pick one that matches your skin color exactly. If you get the color wrong, it will contrast starkly, making you look silly on TV.

If you care about your own image, you can never depend on anyone else to take care of your makeup. I have been in small town TV stations that have rundown equipment, and they have given me great professional makeup applications. And then I have been at the NBC Headquarters at 30 Rockefeller Plaza in New York City for a national broadcast and there was no one there to help me with it. (You can never judge the quality of makeup you will receive by looking at the size of a TV station or market.)

So did I go without?

No, I simply pulled out my own makeup compact and applied it to my face in about one minute. It wasn't quite as good a job as what Dan Rather gets each night, but it worked.

If you think you might be on TV anytime in the next year, go to a local drugstore to purchase your own powder compact. Then, if necessary, all you will have to do before your appearance is pat it on and blend it in so that it's smooth all over. This way you'll look like the best you that you can possibly be.

Smile For The Camera

From kindergarten on, we are taught to smile for still photography cameras. While this may make for some stilted pictures, smiling is a good strategy anytime you are in front of a TV camera.

Most people have a blank, expressionless look on their face when listening to someone else talking. In person, this looks fine. In fact, it would look odd to someone talking to you if you sat there with a big, stupid grin on your face for no reason. However, on television, a blank or flat expression does not look blank. Instead, it looks like a frown. Quite often you will see hotshot business executives or celebrities introduced with great fanfare on CNN or NBC. However, the first thing you notice is that they look glum, bored or detached. It's because they have a blank look on their face while they are busy listening to the host introducing them.

The only way around this is to put, and keep, a slight smile on your face whenever you are in front of a TV camera. I don't mean a gigantic Pat Robertson "send-me-your-Social-Security-check" smile. All you need is a slight smile to look more comfortable, confident and relaxed. Think of it as showing a few teeth and raising your cheeks slightly.

Here is a TV trick: if you smile slightly, it won't look as if you are smiling to the people who watch you on TV, you will simply look more confident and engaging. Remember TV cools you down.

Another trick for the TV camera: keep a slight smile on your face WHILE you are talking. This sounds ridiculous, it feels ridiculous, but it works.

A common reaction I get from clients is, "But TJ, I'm talking about serious issues – we just had a plane crash and 10 employees were killed. I can't smile during a TV interview for a subject like this – people will think I'm an insensitive jerk."

This is an understandable reaction; however, it shows an ignorance of how the camera works. You will look more comfortable, conscientious and caring if you smile slightly EVEN when you are delivering bad news. The camera minimizes everything. It takes a blank look and actually makes it look like a frown, and it takes a smile and makes it appear neutral. So if you want an authoritative, neutral appearance while having to announce bad news, you still need to smile slightly.

When on TV, you should avoid the following involving your mouth:

- Don't lick your lips. This looks lascivious on camera. Make sure you drink plenty of water before your interview so that you won't be tempted to lick your lips during the interview.
- Don't stick your tongue out while you are speaking – this looks serpentine.
- Don't bite your lips – this makes you look nervous.

If you can't remember these do's and don'ts, just remember to keep a slight smile on your face. That will cover up most other potential problems.

Move Your Head

The frozen head is the surest sign that a novice is appearing on TV. The businessperson is so determined to "get the message out" that all of his energy is spent trying to pull a script out of his brain to deliver it before it is forgotten. The result? The executive looks nervous and frozen. The average viewer watching from home or office can't quite put a finger on it, but he or she knows something is wrong with the frozen-headed executive.

It is natural to move your head when you talk. This isn't a new skill you have to go out and learn. If you don't believe me, try watching television with the mute button turned on. Every sitcom actor's head moves. Every soap opera actor's head moves when talking. If you watch the news anchors on CBS,

NBC or ABC with the sound off, you will notice that they move their heads when they talk, too.

Unfortunately, when people get nervous, they stop doing things they normally do, like moving their head. If you are tense or nervous before your TV appearance, you may have to consciously think to yourself during the middle of the interview, "Now I am moving my head to the right and now to the left." This may seem highly contrived, but you will LOOK more natural if you do so.

Here are a few other points to keep in mind regarding moving your head while appearing on TV:

- It is OK to tilt your head occasionally, but don't consistently tilt it to one side. This will make you seem passive and not authoritative.
- Don't make any quick, jerking movements with your head – these will be distracting.
- Feel free to nod your head in agreement or shake your head in disagreement when appropriate.

Head motion, especially a nod of disagreement, can get the attention of TV directors and producers. If, for example, you are appearing on a cable TV news show and another guest is attacking you or saying something with which you strongly disagree, you may want to shake your head in disagreement. The director may then go to a split screen and show your adversary making comments while showing you shaking your head, "No." The net effect is that the audience maybe less inclined to believe what your opponent is saying because your body language is suggesting that it's not true. (Be careful not to overuse this technique or you could be perceived as being highly rude.)

So remember, when it comes to what is above your neck, your mouth is not the only thing that can move and communicate – use your entire head.

Lean Forward To Look Lean

There are many simple, yet not common sense, tips for appearing on TV in the best light possible. For example, you know that you should look comfortable and relaxed when you appear on TV; you don't want to look uptight. But if you sit back and relax in a chair or couch on a TV set, you will look TERRIBLE.

If you sit back and relax, your head will be further away from the camera than your abdomen. Unfortunately, the camera latches on to whatever is closest. If the camera is closer to your gut, it will magnify your stomach. The result? You will look 20–30 pounds heavier than you do in real life. Even if you have six-pack abs, you will look as if you have a large tummy roll. To make matters worse, you will look like you have a double chin, even if you've had more face-lifts than Michael Jackson. So don't lean back in a couch or chair when you are on TV.

Your next option is to sit up perfectly straight, just like your mother taught you when you were in first grade. In this case, your mom's advice won't work. If you sit up perfectly straight while in front of a TV camera, you will look as stiff as a board, nervous, scared and highly uncomfortable. Don't sit up perfectly straight either!

So where does this leave us?

The last – and best – option is to hold yourself up high and lean forward about 15 degrees toward the camera. This will make you appear taller, thinner, younger and leaner, while accentuating your jaw line. Because the camera latches on to whatever is closest, it will now give more prominence to your head and mouth, and less to any excess padding you may have below (a major plus for many well-fed business executives, myself included).

So for seated TV interviews, always lean forward about 15 degrees toward the camera. If you are standing, don't lean forward quite that much or you might fall over. Just make sure you don't stand up too rigidly straight, or you will appear nervous and stiff.

The final thing to remember about your body during a TV interview is to move slightly. Don't remain stiff. You don't want to move around in a quick, jerky fashion, but you do want to exhibit subtle, natural movement. Occasionally move forward, backward and to the side 3 to 6 inches, just as you normally would when having an animated conversation with a friend.

By leaning forward and moving slightly in a full range, you will look your very best in every TV appearance.

Keep Your Tongue In Your Mouth

One of the most annoying things a speaker can do, in person or on television, is stick his or her tongue out while speaking. Why do speakers and people in the media do this?

Several reasons:

- Being nervous can make a speaker do unusual things.
- Being nervous can make the mouth go dry. The tongue then shoots out, licking the lips in search of moisture.
- Being nervous can make the lips go dry, so the tongue shoots out to moisten them.
- Talking louder than normal or with more energy than usual forces air out of the mouth with greater velocity, drying the mouth further. Again, the tongue shoots out in search of water.
- Talking under bright stage or TV lights can also make the speaker hot and thirsty, and the tongue goes into action.

The one thing that tongue-sticker-outers all have in common is that they have no idea that they stick out their tongues when speaking. They are always shocked when I point out their darting tongues on video. People do it unconsciously.

Unfortunately, this tongue darting is highly noticeable to the live or TV audience. When a speaker or TV interviewee sticks out his or her tongue, the audience may conclude that the speaker is nervous, uncertain, tentative or anxious. They may even consider the speaker as having dubious moral character.

Is it fair for audiences to make all of these harsh judgments?

Of course not, but they do.

Fortunately, this is an easy problem to correct once you become aware of it. For starters, drink plenty of room-temperature water before you speak or go on TV. Drink more than you usually do, and drink even if you are not thirsty. Also, avoid salty foods before you speak; these can increase your thirst. Additionally, avoid coffee, alcohol or any other drinks that could dehydrate you. Next, be conscious of what your mouth is doing and where your tongue is going. Make a concerted effort to keep your tongue inside your mouth. Finally, have a glass of water nearby while you speak. If you are giving a 30-minute speech, there is nothing wrong with stopping every 8 to 10 minutes for a sip of water. If you are on a TV panel discussion, have a glass of water within reach so that you can drink during the commercial breaks.

Remember, you will never become a master communicator until you learn to master your tongue.

What Do I Do With My Hands?

Several times each week, I have speech and media training clients who come into my training studio who express themselves in an extraordinarily passionate, confident manner. Everything about their voice, body and hand gestures conveys confidence.

Then I put the video camera on them so that they can practice a speech or media interview. Instantly, it's as if their arms have become lifeless appendages that were sewn onto their torsos in the middle of the night – as devoid of nerve endings as a Punch-'NJudy doll. Their voices become flat, boring and monotone. They sound and move like zombies, and if their hands move at all, it is to assume the military at-ease position or a fig-leaf pose.

Inevitably, the client says to me, "What do I do with my hands? I never know what to do with my hands when I'm speaking."

What should you do with your hands when you are speaking?

There is a lot of misinformation about this subject. Someone somewhere told speakers that they should not gesture with their hands – that they would seem unprofessional – and somehow this myth caught on. Unfortunately, this is the worst advice any speaker can ever receive. Confident, comfortable people always speak while gesturing with their hands. Nervous people rarely ever move their hands. If you want to appear to be confident and comfortable, move your hands. When you stop moving your hands, your body also moves less, creating a more boring visual experience for your audience.

However, the fundamental reason you should move your hands when you speak to audiences or in front of TV cameras is that this is what you do the rest of the time when you speak naturally. In fact, most people are hardwired to speak with their hands every time they open their mouth.

Susan Goldin-Meadow, author of Hearing Gesture: How Our Hands Help Us Think, points out clinical studies that reveal that even deaf and blind infants gesture when they are making sounds. Moving our hands when we make sounds from our mouth is how we human beings are programmed!

Because they are nervous, many presenters do not gesture when they are in front of an audience or a TV camera. And this is the beginning of a process that destroys their entire presentation. When they keep their hands from making their natural movements, they end up tensing up their entire arms. This tension spreads throughout the rest of their body until it ultimately reaches their vocal cords.

The result? A voice that used to sound rich, resonant, energetic and conversational now sounds dull, flat, monotone, tense and low in volume. At this point, the speech is destined for failure, and it all started as a chain reaction triggered by not using natural hand gestures.

Do you think that you don't normally gesture with your hands when you speak?

You are wrong.

Most of my clients think they don't either. All I do is videotape them after they are through presenting a formal speech, when they don't realize they are being taped. Then I simply fast-forward to the part of the tape during which they were being secretly recorded. Invariably, they are gesturing a great deal, and, accordingly, moving their arms, body and head, sounding 1,000 times better than their formal speech a few minutes prior.

That always settles that argument.

As you try to add hand gestures back into your repertoire, the key to looking good is to move naturally. Don't consciously try to jab one finger or clench your fist with your thumb on top. Don't consciously gesture with one hand while keeping the other in your pocket. Instead, just forget about your hands and use them the way you normally do.

Befriend Your Host

For years I have stressed that you should be friendly to your on-air hosts. After all, these hosts have been invited guests in people's living rooms, bedrooms and offices, sometimes on a daily basis for years. The audience has a bond with the host, not with you.

For that reason it is a good idea to address the host by name occasionally (but don't start every sentence using the host's name – that gets annoying). Similarly, I always used to advocate shaking hands with your host at the end of an interview segment. This visually demonstrates a link between the host and you. Ideally, some of the goodwill the audience has toward the host will rub off on you. Plus, this is the last impression the audience will have of you, being gracious and acting friendly with the host.

Alas, this advice is no longer applicable on all TV interview formats. Recently, I was being profiled on Bloomberg TV, the business network, in a taped interview. At the conclusion of the interview, I reached over to shake the hand of the interviewer and he reluctantly shook it.

Then the host said, "Cut, we will have to do that over. Sorry, TJ, but our corporate policies forbid us from shaking hands with guests on the air. After all of the conflict-of-interest scandals in the financial world in recent years, our policy makers have decided it looks too much like hosts and guests are buddy-buddy insiders. Not what we want our viewers to think."

I had to admit I had never thought of it that way.

"I'm sorry," was all I could muster.

Fortunately, the host had to re-tape only the final five seconds of the show, so there was no big waste of time or damage to the interview due to my faux pas.

The new rule of thumb is NOT to shake hands on financial news programs on any of the networks, unless the host shakes hands with you first. For local TV interview programs that are live, or recorded as if they were live, I would still err on the side of shaking hands with the host.

Be A Name Dropper

If you are being interviewed by a television reporter for an edited story, be sure to be a name dropper – just make sure the name you drop is the reporter's name.

For example: "Stone, it was the most terrifying night of my life."

Guess what? Stone Phillips of NBC News is more likely to use that quote. Why?

Because his name is in it.

Remember, TV reporters don't have big egos – they have HUGE egos. They like seeing and hearing their name. The more you use their name, the more the reporters can inject themselves into the story. This may be a sad commentary on the state of TV journalism, but that's not our concern here. Your role is to get your message out to a TV audience, and if interjecting a reporter's name every third sentence helps you do that, what do you care?

It is in the reporter's self-interest to become a bigger part of the story. The most highly paid TV journalists in the world are people like Mike Wallace. A story by Mike Wallace is more about Mike Wallace than it is about any one story subject. That's not knocking Mike Wallace; it's just a reality. So use this reality to your own advantage by using a reporter's name before you deliver a sound bite on your message – it will increase the odds of your getting the exact quote you want.

But just remember, this works only with TV reporters. Print journalists don't care because their editors never allow a reporter's name to make it into print.

Prepping For Prime Time

If only you could get on The Oprah Winfrey Show or 60 Minutes, then you'd be rich and famous and all of your problems would be solved, right?

Maybe, maybe not.

Although there are things you can do to greatly enhance your chances of getting on wildly popular shows with huge audiences, doing the following will NOT increase your chances of getting major placements:

- calling the shows' producers every two days, telling them that you are the greatest thing since Low-fat frozen double mocha
- calling your publicist and threatening to fire him or her if he or she doesn't get you on Oprah in the next 72 hours

- mailing yet another copy of your book (the 14th copy in 43 days) to the host or producer
- calling your brother-in-law's uncle, who works in advertising at Procter & Gamble, and asking him to put some pressure on the show or suggest that ads will be pulled

Businesspeople and authors use all of these tactics regularly, and they are definitely counterproductive.

The best way to get on these national-level shows is to be incredibly interesting and good on TV at the local level. Producers for the big national shows want to see you on videotape in front of real audiences before they risk putting you on their shows. So every time you go on a local cable TV access show or get interviewed for the local morning show on the NBC affiliate in Tallahassee, Florida, it could be the steppingstone to the big time.

It is critical to watch a videotape of your performance after each TV appearance and get feedback from other people as well. Ask someone you trust to rip you apart. The best critique will include specific suggestions on what to improve. You should see regular improvement over time.

Finally, put together a demonstration ("demo") tape that consists of the clips of your best appearances on local TV. With that in hand, you now have a door opener for getting you booked on national TV.

If you try all of that and you still don't succeed, too bad. Keep doing more local TV and keep revising your demo tape until it gets better and better. If all you do is sit back and wait for Oprah to call you, you certainly aren't getting any better at your TV communication skills. And when Oprah's producers do call you and ask you what TV shows you have been on in the last six months, you don't want to have to say none.

So get out there and do as many small-market TV shows you can find. Get tapes of yourself. Review. Critique. Improve. And then keep your "TV appearances greatest hits" video handy at all times.

Tip #813

"Don't wear stripes, herringbone, small intricate designs or flashy
jewelry on TV. They are hard for a camera to pick up."

From: *1001 Ways to Wow the Media and Speaking Audiences*

Chapter 4:
Creating And Conveying
Your Media Message

You never want to go into a media interview, whether in person or over the phone, without a clear-cut media message in mind. I define a media message as something you can say in 30 seconds that includes the three key points you want to convey to your audience. You have a plan or a goal for everything else you do in business; you should have such a goal for media interviews, too.

"But TJ, there is no time. Reporters call me directly and I have to answer them off the top of my head."

No, you don't. Whenever a reporter calls you, the first thing you should do is find out what the interview topic is. Then ask the reporter, "What is your deadline?" Inform the reporter that you are on another call or in a meeting (even if it is with yourself), but that you will be happy to grant the interview before the deadline. The reporter's deadline may be in 10 minutes, but at least that will give you 5 minutes to prepare your message.

Never ever, ever talk to reporters without giving yourself time to prepare your message. This will not only save you time in the long run, but it will also help you get your message out more effectively, as your interviews will be shorter and more productive.

Stop Worrying About The Questions

The first thing the average embattled politician or corporate executive does to prepare for a media interview or press conference is to brainstorm with his or her staff to come up with all of the questions reporters might ask. This process might take hours or even days, and it is a complete waste of time!

I'm not saying that questions don't matter; they do. People think that media consultants like me tell our clients to ignore the questions completely and just stick to the prepared message. However, that's not the recommended strategy either.

You do want to brainstorm and determine the four or five most obvious questions that will come up during the interview, plus the one or two questions you think would be hardest for you to answer. But here is the reality: you will never know all of the questions that will be asked because you have no control over the interviewer or his or her questions.

What you do have control over are your answers, and you have total control over your basic message. Most people go into an interview without a firm, clear, simple, easy-to-understand message. This is their downfall – not a lack of knowledge regarding the questions.

When you focus so much of your time on possible questions, you are entering into an entirely reactive relationship with the interviewer. You are giving all of the power to the journalist. This is a defensive position.

You want to enter the interview with a well-thought out message that answers the most basic questions that might come up during a discussion of the subject. Then you want to use your answers as a bridge back to your main message.

Too many of my clients obsess over so-called tough questions that could come up. There are no tough questions. For any question there are exactly two answers: either you know the answer and you put it forth simply and articulately, or you don't know the answer and you say, "I don't know," and you then steer the conversation back to relevant information that you do know.

Never tell a reporter, "That's a good question." If I am a reporter, I think all of my questions are brilliant. You have now implied that some of my other questions are less than Pulitzer-Prize material – an outrage! Additionally, there is no such thing as a stupid question, an ignorant question or a leading question. Why? Because unless it is live TV or radio, the readers, viewers or listeners never get to hear or see the questions.

However, there is such a thing as a stupid answer, a bad answer or a dumb answer. Your answers will be staring back at you for eternity – so make them good. This is where you should focus exclusively – on your answers.

Past May Repeat

Positive
Answer most basic Questions
Short
Top Three Only

Media
Audience
You

Results
Everything You Have To Say
Problem
Engaging and Unique
Accomplishments/Solutions
Tight and Simple

At Media Training Worldwide we have created a system for creating messages called PAST MAY REPEAT. This Acronym will steer you toward all of the points you need to focus on when coming up with your media message.

The Power Of The Positive

When you are constructing your media messages, make sure to come up with points that are entirely positive about yourself. There will be plenty of other people – competitors or journalists – willing to say negative things about you. You can't control that, but you don't have to make your detractors' job any easier.

It is human nature to be drawn to people and ideas that are framed in a positive fashion. This doesn't mean you should sugarcoat issues or dissemble, but it IS essential to frame your arguments in a clean, simple, well-focused manner without getting bogged down in, "On the one hand this . . . and on the other hand that . . ."

When formulating your media messages, sort out those that are completely positive from those that contain mixed or negative elements.

The Power of Positive Thinking may come across as glib clichés when coming from another generic motivational speaker, but when you start to open your mouth in front of the news media, make sure your message is 100 percent positive about you. You may have to define a problem or even criticize others, but don't be critical of yourself in any manner.

Answering The Basic Questions

A good media message answers the most basic, obvious questions that you think will come up when a reporter interviews you on a certain subject. It's a good idea to have answers to who, what, where, when, why and how, plus other questions you know will be asked. A good 30- to 60-second three-part message will answer these questions without the reporter even having to ask them. By supplying answers easily and quickly to the obvious questions, you are showing the reporter respect while building your own credibility.

BUT . . .

Don't go overboard. Many executives and politicians with whom I have worked over the years had previously spent hours and hours brainstorming dozens, even hundreds, of complex, hypothetical questions. And yet these same people never had a clear, simple and easy-to-understand basic message on the topic.

Ultimately, you have to realize that there are an unlimited number of questions that can be asked by reporters. As newsmakers, spokespeople and experts, we have ZERO control over the questioning process. We have 100 percent control (ideally) over what comes out of our own mouth. That's why I believe interviewees should spend 90 percent of their time refining their message and their sound bites, and 10 percent of their time worrying about which questions are going to be asked, instead of the other way around.

I am NOT saying that questions don't matter and that you should just ignore the questions and say whatever you want. I'm just pointing out that it makes more sense to focus on your role in the process. Your role is to have interesting, quotable answers. It is the reporter's job to ask the questions. If you do your job of coming up with interesting and newsworthy messages related to the topic at hand, this will make you a media success. If, however, you successfully predict the questions you will be asked, but your answers are reactive, defensive, overly complex or muddled, you will not get any credit from the reporter, readers, viewers or listeners. Worse, you will have failed at your one true objective: getting YOUR message out.

Keep It Short

A good media message is short. Ideally, you should be able to say everything you deem important on a particular subject in 30 seconds or fewer.

If it takes you longer than 30 seconds to get your message out, you really haven't applied enough discipline to the editing process. If you are still talking after 30 seconds, you are likely going on to the fourth, fifth or sixth message point – save those for your speeches, not your media interviews.

Do whatever it takes to make your message short and sweet. If you have to tape a picture of Napoleon or Danny DeVito to your computer, then do it. Once you run over in a media interview, you lose your focus and your ability to control your message.

During his presidential campaign in 1980, Ronald Reagan's message to the media was that, as President, he wanted to cut taxes, strengthen defense and restore traditional values. Bill Clinton's message in 1992 was that he wanted to create more jobs and improve health care. The one thing both messages have in common is that they can be delivered in fewer than 30 seconds.

Whether you liked or disliked either man or their policies, they were both successful, in part, because they learned to keep their media messages short and to just a few points. Unless your job is more important than being President of the United States, you would be well advised to keep your media messages short, too.

Creating Your Media Message

When you are creating your media message, make sure to brainstorm for every possible idea. Write down every possible point you could say on a subject. During this process, it is essential that you suspend all of your analytical and critical thinking. Instead, just try to be as creative as possible, tossing out as many ideas as you can.

I recommend brainstorming for ideas before the actual interview with a reporter, the point at which the results will be seen or heard by the rest of the world. The beauty of tossing out a dumb idea during a private brainstorming session is that it can not hurt you. And if you write it down and consciously scratch it off the list, you are less likely to have that dumb idea spill out of your mouth during the real interview.

Do not try to save time during this process. Let it all hang out. If you are working with a bunch of colleagues, encourage each person to toss in some ideas. If anyone tries to shoot down an idea, tell him or her to stifle it. The brainstorming process needs to be unrestricted.

Come up with at least one full page of possible message points. Then take a look at them all at once. Now begins the editing process. Someone is going to be the editor of your story. It could be the journalist, producer or editor who doesn't particularly care about you or your business, or it could be you. If you go into the interview and you dump out all 57 message points that you have on your subject, the journalist gets to edit your messages down to three or so, and he or she will probably select the three points you care about the least, which don't even make sense unless five other points that didn't make it into the story are included. This is the way most newsmakers edit their stories, and that's why people waste a lot of time complaining about the news media and their so-called biases.

However, if you choose to edit your own story, you are in control. With this approach, you look at all 57 of your brainstorming points and rank them in order of importance. Go through and check off the ones that strike you as absolutely essential. Then scratch off the ones you can live without. If you are not sure about some, put a question mark next to them. You may realize that some points are similar or that they speak to the same theme, so you can condense them into one point. After the first round, you might have checks next to nine message points and question marks next to four.

Keep scratching off, connecting, questioning and checking. Ultimately, you want to end up with three main message points. You should be able to say all three message points in about 30 seconds. If it takes you longer than that, you really haven't narrowed your message down to three points; you still have five, six or more points.

Don't be greedy! If you go into a media interview with the goal of trying to communicate more than three main message points, chances are, you will fail. Have three clear, simple, easy-to understand points for your next media encounter and you will be primed for success.

The Power Of Three

Anytime you are communicating to people through the news media, it is crucial to narrow your message down to no more than three points. "Why three?" you and my clients ask. The answer is, "I don't really know."

I am certain of this though – if you try to communicate more than three ideas in an interview or even in a series of interviews, you will end up confusing audiences, readers and reporters. If you communicate 17 points, a reporter is likely to focus on two or three of your points anyway, probably ones that don't even make sense unless people hear the first 10 that didn't make it into the story.

So why not have just one or two points? That's too monotonous and boring. The reporter or talk-show host will think you are a simpleton if you can only talk about one or two points. Hence, the beauty of three.

The most successful communicators of all time know and live by the rule of three. Presidential candidates are interviewed thousands of times during an election year. Books, documentaries and magazine covers are devoted to telling you everything you could possibly want to know about what a candidate will do once in office.

But savvy presidential candidates know that most people don't vote on the basis of timber rights policy. As previously mentioned, when Ronald Reagan ran for president in 1980, he stuck to three main message points. As President, he would

1. cut taxes
2. strengthen defense
3. balance the budget

You might not have agreed with his message. You might not think he took action on all three (budget balancing?). But it is undeniable that he had a clear and simple message that he stuck to, and the people who voted for him understood his message.

Quick – name the three main points made in Jimmy Carter's 1980 campaign.

I can't do it either.

In 1992, Bill Clinton ran for President using these three main themes:

1. Change versus the status quo.
2. It's the economy, stupid.
3. Don't forget healthcare.

Is there any doubt that his message got through? True, there were many other messages swirling around Clinton during that campaign, but Clinton stuck to his key ideas using remarkable discipline.

Quick – name the three top three themes of the George Bush's 1992 reelection campaign.

Again, I can't either.

When communicating via the media, don't get greedy. Stick to three message points.

Reporters Are Distracted

My media training clients regularly ask me, "TJ, why must I repeat my three-part message so often during a phone interview? Isn't once or twice enough?"

No, it is not enough!

When reporters are interviewing you over the phone, they are doing a million other things at the same time. They are answering email, surfing the web, receiving instant messages, watching CNN, listening to their editor yell at them and, yes, trying to write down what you are saying. Plus, they are waiting for that call from Alan Greenspan (and know that they will dump you in a second if he calls).

In short, they are distracted. They probably aren't going to get what you are talking about the first or even second time you mention it. They certainly aren't going to notice that you are repeating yourself.

So repeat your same basic message over and over again. Just make sure you don't say it the same way, word for word each time. As long as you mix up the order, give different examples or thread elements of their questions through your message points, most reporters will never notice that you are repeating yourself. And those that do will appreciate that you have given thought to what is most important.

So don't feel embarrassed about having a strong, compelling message and sticking to it throughout your interview. Of course, this doesn't mean you are going to dodge questions. You will answer all questions – briefly – and then you will bridge back to your main themes. This will ensure your message makes it to the final cut so that you can get what you want into the story.

What Does The Media Want?

When creating your media messages, it is crucial that you consider all possible constituencies. One group you need to think about is the media. Will the reporters to whom you are talking find your message interesting?

You may come up with several messages that are short and positive that highlight your accomplishments. For example, it might be important to you and even to some of your customers that your company has been in existence for 212 years. However, it is highly unlikely that anyone in the news media is going to care that you have been around for 212 years. If the media don't care, they won't put it into the story. If you know in advance that a certain message point isn't going to make it into the story, why waste time even trying? If you try to force a message point on a reporter that is of no interest to him or her as a journalist, all you are doing is destroying your credibility and making it harder for you to get your remaining message points into the story.

So after you have brainstormed for all of your possible message points, go through each one, one at a time, and ask yourself, "If I were a reporter, would I find this point interesting enough to tell my readers, viewers or listeners about this?" If the answer isn't an enthusiastic "yes," then scratch it off the list.

Does The Audience Care?

When crafting your media messages, consider what will appeal to your audience. There are some messages that may be of great interest to reporters, but not to readers, viewers or listeners. For example, political reporters love to write stories on campaign finance reform, political fundraising and insider strategy conflicts. But news consumers and voters don't care about this stuff AT ALL. So if you waste time pandering to reporters on these issues, you do yourself and your campaign no good.

It might be important to you and everyone in your company that you have been certified by internationally recognized safety standards organizations. But, chances are, none of your customers or clients find this particularly interesting or relevant to them, therefore this information would not make for a good message point in your interview with The Wall Street Journal. So if you want to brag about your compliance with ISO standards, save that message for your in-house corporate newsletter or the employee section of your web site, but don't tell the world if the world doesn't care.

To craft a good media message, it is crucial to take your audience into consideration. If your message isn't of critical importance to your audience, get a new message or find a new audience. (It's probably easier to find a new message.)

What Do You Want?

Many executives and politicians spend so much time trying to figure out what reporters want in the form of answers to questions that they lose sight of the primary goal: communicating good things about themselves and their organizations. Of course, you have to take into consideration what is of interest to the media and to your audience, but don't forget the most important constituency in the messaging process: yourself.

Whether you are facing a crisis or the local society reporter wants to write a puff piece on you, you should always be on the offensive, advancing positive things about yourself. Once you get in a reactive mode, you are stuck in a defensive position. In this capacity you spend all of your energy trying to avoid getting hurt or trying to minimize pain.

Why be so pessimistic? No matter how cynical the reporter is or how negative the story may be, you always have a chance at getting some of your positive message points out. But if you never try . . .

Remember, if you know that the media wants to hear a certain message from you and your audience wants to hear a certain message from you, don't give it to them unless it is also a message that you absolutely want communicated. If your message doesn't appeal to all three constituencies, it isn't a winning message point, so scratch it.

Results Are Key

A good media message talks about results. What have you done? What is the pot of gold at the end of your rainbow? When you are touting your strengths to the media, don't get mired in theory and abstract concepts. Instead, talk about the results of your genius, hard work or other talents. Don't make reporters guess or probe in order for these to accidentally spill out. Place your results right up front as a part of your 30-second, three-part message.

Remember, it's not bragging if you have the results to back up your statement. So if your actions have created results and your successful strategies can be repeated, you should promote them by incorporating them into your basic media messages. If you don't talk about your positive results, no one else will.

Say Everything You HAVE To Say

A good media message should contain everything that you absolutely, positively have to say about a topic – not everything you could say, might say or want to say. You should be able to deliver your entire message in 30 to 45 seconds; obviously, you can't say everything you know from A to Z on the subject, but you can start with A, then jump to J and conclude with Z.

If you think that you have a great, clear, three-part message, but you find that you keep coming back to additional points when you rehearse your interviews, that means it's time to rewrite your message points. If there is something you feel highly compelled to say about a subject, and you feel it is in your best interest to communicate it, it had better be included in your basic, three-part message.

Remember, there is a big difference between saying everything you have to say versus everything you'd like to say on a subject. Do not confuse being the subject of a media interview with writing a column, giving a speech or posting a white paper on your web site. Figure out what you HAVE to say and then stick to it.

Part of becoming a true master of the media is developing the discipline of testing your messages by practicing and rehearsing in front of colleagues before you undergo the actual interview. The trick is having the courage to throw away some message points to make room for other more important ones after you have refined them. Once you go into an interview, you don't want to have any confusion about your message. At that moment you are past the point when you can make any more changes.

What Is Your Problem?

A good media message addresses problems. What problem are you solving? Reporters are – at their most fundamental level – storytellers, and good stories always contain conflict and problems.

What is your problem? More specifically, what is the problem you are solving for other people? If you are in business, what problem do you solve for which people are willing to pay you money? If you are in politics, what problem in society are you trying to fix?

A strong media message spells out a problem in a clear-cut, compelling and possibly visual manner. By laying this out, you create anticipation for your solutions.

If your message contains nothing but problems, you are nothing but a complainer. But if you can articulate a specific problem and immediately follow it up with a compelling solution, then you are on your way to becoming a master communicator.

Make It Engaging!

You want your media message to be engaging and unique. After all, when speaking to the NEWS media, you should have something new to say. It simply won't do to spout out last year's marketing slogan and expect a reporter to find that interesting enough to include in a story.

When you are testing potential media messages, make sure that at least one of them is genuinely new news or that it at least has a new spin. Reporters are paid to come up with new stories for their readers, viewers or listeners. You are of no use to them if you are handing out old material.

Of course, there are very few entirely new ideas under the sun, but there are new combinations of ideas that can form a newsworthy message. Be sure to put a new package on your ideas before presenting them to the news media. This will increase the odds that you are taken seriously and that your message finds a place in front of a larger audience.

Your message doesn't have to be funny or extreme or outlandish, but it does need a novel twist. So don't make the mistake of trying to push last month's ad copy from a brochure on unsuspecting reporters. Unfortunately, these reporters are expecting much more from you – and you must deliver the goods. Come up with a new angle for your messages.

Accomplishments And Solutions

Use your media message to highlight your accomplishments and solutions. What have you actually done? If you landed on the moon, remind people. If you aren't just a start-up company and have been around awhile, what is your track record? The past often does predict the future. If a reporter asks you about what is going to happen in the future regarding a certain topic, don't be shy in talking about relevant accomplishments from the recent or semi-recent past.

Is there a new problem facing customers in your industry? What solutions did you come up with in the past? Reminding people through the media is a great way of positioning yourself as the problem-solver to turn to – now and in the future. So make sure that at least one of your media messages extols your accomplishments and solutions.

Make Your Message Tight And Simple

While your media message should be positive, solution oriented and accomplishment laden, it also needs to be tight and simple. It should fit together easily, like a children's LEGO® toy.

While some of your messages have all the right elements, they may be too long or complex to fully explain in less than five minutes (remember, you only have about 30 seconds). In that case, it is better to save those messages for a speech, when you have a captive audience, a white paper for your web site, an op-ed column, or even a book or special report. Don't try to convey a complex message point during an interview.

It's not (necessarily) that reporters are stupid. It's just that they don't know as much about your subject as you do, or they have to follow 50 other industries as well. In some cases, the reporter does know as much as you do and gets your story "right," but that reporter's editor doesn't understand your message, so in the process of editing and ostensibly making things clearer to the readers, viewers or listeners, your message gets distorted beyond reality.

Complexity is your enemy when dealing with reporters. Focus on simple, easy-to-understand media messages. If you have four important messages to communicate and one is a lot more complex than the other three, cut the complex one and keep the other three.

There is a time and a place for everything. Wait until you have a live customer in front of you for a face-to-face presentation before you attempt to communicate your most complex messages. When it comes to using the news media, keep your messages tight and simple, and you can't go wrong.

Avoid The Weasel Words

Many business communicators lard up their speeches with jargon and weasel words. The result? They sound like bureaucratic stooges.

Your goal when dealing with the media is to communicate a message in the clearest and simplest manner possible, while at the same time building your reputation as a strong and forceful communicator. Strong and forceful are relative terms, so if you use all of the same buzzwords that everyone else does, you will always seem mediocre. Many businesspeople acquire their bad rhetorical habits at some point during their second year of business school or after having attended their third annual board of directors meeting.

Here are some of the worst offenders:

- "Going forward . . ." What an utterly useless phrase. Use "in the future" instead. You wouldn't tell your teenage son, "Going forward, please keep your room straight," so why use it in a speech or interview? The sole purpose for using a phrase like "going forward" in a speech is to create the impression that you are saying something fancier than you actually are. So please, going forward, never use the phrase "going forward."

- "If you will." People tack this phrase onto the back of a sentence as if to say, "Look at this most original and brilliant insight I have just come up with. It will require you to change your whole conception of the universe, if you will be so kind as to indulge me in this mind-thought experiment." Pretentious drivel! Imagine a trap door, if you will, that will spring open and devour you if you ever use the phrase "if you will" in a public speech.

- "As it were." See above.

There is nothing wrong with using specialized language to convey complex concepts to sophisticated audiences, but that is not what many business communicators do. Instead, they use complex phrases to communicate simple concepts because they are under the delusion that this makes them sound more professional. The more simply and conversationally you can speak, regardless of the topic's complexity, the more likely your audiences will understand, respect and appreciate you and your message.

Daily Video, Audio & Text

TJ Walker explains the principles of speaking to the media and giving better presentations in short video and audio clips.

Visit www.speakcast.com to listen and watch

Chapter 5:
Fielding Questions

Answering questions from a reporter is NOT like answering questions from a friend, colleague, boss, employee, investor or family member. It is NOT like having a real conversation. (Live TV and radio interviews are slightly more like live conversations, but even still they are not exactly the same.) In a real conversation, you have context, you understand the context and usually your audience understands the context. If you are explaining something to an employee, you can reference something you said five minutes earlier. If you are answering a question from your boss and he stops to take a phone call when you are mid-sentence, you understand that you need to stop talking because he won't be able to hear anything you say while he is talking on the phone, and it won't have an impact.

If you are giving a speech, you can see if most of the audience is paying attention. You can also build one idea on another, referencing something you said earlier in order to highlight a complex idea. You don't have that luxury when you are talking to the media.

In a real life conversation, if your son says to you, "You are the worst mom in the whole world because you won't let me play with firecrackers the way all my friends get to," it may be fine to preface your response with, "Son, I understand that you think I am the worst mom in the whole world for not letting you play with firecrackers, but . . ."

However, what are good conversational skills in the real world can DESTROY you in the media world.

Many people who are great speakers and one-on-one communicators never make the adjustment to being good media communicators because they don't understand this one key concept: YOU DON'T CONTROL THE CONTEXT OF A CONVERSATION WITH THE MEDIA. Because you can't control the context, it fundamentally alters how you must talk and answer questions. Unlike every other conversation in life, in a media conversation, every single idea you utter will be judged on its own, not within the context of what you said before or after it.

Why is this so? Because you aren't actually having a conversation with the reporter. You are having a conversation with the readers, viewers or listeners of that reporter, and you don't know which of your ideas are going to make the final cut. Consequently, you must take a radically more disciplined approach to how you answer questions in a media interview. Some pointers follow:

Open Media Rap

Open With A Short Answer To A Specific Question
Pick One Of Many Questions
Eyes On Message Points
Never Repeat Negative Words Or Assumptions

Move To Message Points
Eliminate Complexity
Delete Database Of Knowledge
I Don't Know
Always Hold Up Questions To Light

Rewrite Questions To Suit You
Aim For All Three Message Points
Positive Answers Only

Media Training Worldwide has created a system for answering questions, the OPEN MEDIA RAP. This system will provide you with a framework for dealing with reporters' questions.

Open With A Short Answer

Once you have a media message, you still must answer questions, but how do you do that without losing control of the interview? You don't want to dodge questions or simply repeat the same message over and over. Members of the media will think you are a moron and will therefore not quote you or use you as a future news source.

You must answer questions, but do so with an agenda and a framework of operating principles. For starters, if a reporter asks you a question that is not directly related to one of your three main message points, guess what? You still have to answer it.

The reporter may ask you about a subject which you know a great deal, only you have already decided it is not one of your main messages on this topic. The average media novice will say, "What the heck?" and then pontificate for 10 minutes on the subject. By now, the reporter has forgotten your main message and will probably never come back to it again.

The trick is to open with a direct, brief answer to any question the reporter asks. Answer the question, but do it in about 10 seconds. Then bridge to the most relevant message point that you have prepared in advance. You need to have the discipline to restrain yourself from talking at length on a subject about which you may know a lot, and for which you may even have great passion. It's not your job to show people how smart you are, and you must be able to pass up occasional opportunities to "educate" reporters. The art in this is giving just enough information to the reporters so that they don't feel you are dodging, WHILE making a logical and graceful bridge to one of your points. Then you can talk for another 20 seconds or so on your main points.

Picking Your Poison

Sometimes a reporter will bombard you with three, four, even five questions in a row. This may be a strategy to rattle you and make you crumble. More often, this is not some grand strategy on the part of reporter. Instead, the questions-in-a-bunch simply reflects the reporter's disorganized thought process regarding that topic at that moment.

As the interviewee, it is in your best interest to think like a strategic communicator when this happens, rather than a scintillating conversationalist. A scintillating conversationalist picks the most interesting question to answer, preferably one that will allow him or her to show a breadth and depth of knowledge. Next, the scintillating conversationalist tries to be helpful, well organized, all-encompassing and a bit professorial by saying something like, "Let me take your fourth question first, your third question second," etc. This is how a lot of normal, intelligent, rational people speak; however, it is an extraordinarily counterproductive strategy if your goal is to get your message out through the media.

The skilled communicator never loses sight of the primary objective of the interview: getting the message out of his or her mouth and into the final story. This should color every decision and thought process throughout the interview. So when a reporter tosses out multiple questions at once, the skilled communicator is thinking only the following thought: "What is the ONE question of all those just asked that leads most quickly and easily back to one of my three message points?" That is the only thought going on in our media master's head. The skilled communicator is NOT thinking any of the following questions:

- "Which question is easiest to answer?"
- "Which question allows me to showcase my knowledge base the best?"
- "Which question is intellectually challenging?"
- "In which order should I answer the questions?"

The skilled media communicator doesn't worry about the order in which to answer the questions because he or she is only going to answer one question: the one that leads most easily back to central message points.

That doesn't mean the media master is afraid to answer the other questions or is trying to dodge them. If the reporter wants to re-ask particular questions, that's OK. But half the time the reporter won't do so because he or she will now be focused on asking follow-up questions based on the messages put forth in the previous answer. In this way the media master has successfully gained control of the interview.

Eyes On Your Message

Many business leaders in the news do a good job of delivering their message to the media – the first time they speak in the interview. But then they never return to their message during the rest of the interview.

What to do?

The answer is to keep your eyes on your message – throughout the entire interview. When I tell my trainees this, they think that I am speaking figuratively. I'm not.

In the case of a newspaper, trade publication or radio interview conducted over the phone, I strongly recommend that you have your three message points typed up on a piece of paper in front of you. Then STARE AT YOUR MESSAGE POINTS THROUGHOUT THE INTERVIEW.

If you prefer, keep your message points on your computer screen, but literally have them in your line of sight at all times. We human beings tend to spit out what goes in. So if you are sitting at your desk talking on the phone and your desk is covered with tons of reports, newspapers, graphs and books, this means that a lot of that stuff will come out of your mouth during the course of an interview.

If the interview is conducted over the phone, you get no extra credit for looking up during the interview or speaking from memory. As long as you don't sound like you are reading a script for the very first time, there is nothing wrong with having your head down and staring at your message notes throughout the interview.

Obviously, you can't do this if you are being interviewed in person for television. However, even then, you can be looking at your 3" x 5" card of message points right before the interview, on the way to the interview, during your makeup session and during commercial breaks.

For many interviewees, the tendency is to use the remaining moments before an interview to come up with more facts, messages and answers to an infinite number of potential questions. The time for that is past. Just prior to and certainly once you are in the interview, you should look at one thing and one thing only: your three simple message points.

"I Am Not A Crook"

When you are in an interview, avoid repeating any negative words or assumptions used by the reporter. The reporter gets to use any words he or she wants when asking questions, and you get to use any words you want when answering questions. Don't let a reporter or a talk-show host choose your words for you. When former President Nixon said, "I am not a crook," the only thing he accomplished was giving people the impression that he was a crook.

Your goal is to communicate positive message points about yourself, your company or your organization. The moment you repeat negative words or assumptions during an interview, you give reporters the opportunity to accurately quote you saying negative things.

Example:
Reporter to TJ, "Mr. Walker, isn't it true that you always teach people to lie, obfuscate and dissemble when talking to reporters?"

Walker to reporter, "Of course, I don't always teach people to lie and obfuscate. We at Media Training Worldwide teach executives and spokespeople to communicate positive messages about themselves while answering reporters' questions. We teach people how to understand the goals and tactics of reporters in order to communicate messages in a graceful manner. At the same time, we teach (blah, blah, blah for another 10 minutes on how great we are) . . ."

Guess what the only quote will be from me in tomorrow's newspaper? TJ Walker, president of Media Training Worldwide, confessed, "I don't always teach people to lie and obfuscate." End of quote and there will be no other quotes from me. Can I complain about being quoted out of context? Sure, but so what?

Nobody cares. The reporter quoted me accurately; I have nobody to blame but myself.

In a normal conversation with a friend, family member or colleague, it is quite effective to repeat the negatives in a question; this shows the person with whom you are talking that you are listening and respecting his or her concerns. For example, "Yes, son, I understand that you feel that your mother and I are too strict, and it is horribly unfair that we won't let you stay out until 3 a.m., but . . ." This conversational style is appropriate with family, but it would be disastrous if you used this technique with the media.

Normal, intelligent, rational, logical people feel the need to rebut false premises before bridging to positive message points. In the business world, this works. Don't do this with the media! Do not rebut premises. Do not restate negatives. Do not say what isn't true. Instead, say what IS true, what IS positive, what IS important to you. Then nobody will think you are a crook.

Move To Your Message Points

In every interview you reach a point when you have to give a preliminary, short answer to a question. You answer just enough so that no fair-minded person can accuse you of dodging the question. So what do you do now? You have a choice. You can go more and more deeply into your knowledge database and give a fuller and richer answer, or you can move back to your original key message points.

The media master moves back to the message points. At any point during your interview, you are either moving toward your message points or you are moving away from them. Once you head away, it is exceedingly hard to turn back. Don't lose your focus on your message points. Move toward them—not instantly, but don't take too long either. Skilled media communicators learn to fight the urge to show off expertise. Instead, the media master uses his or her cunning to restate original message points, giving new examples, facts or twists. While the packaging may be different, the core message points remain the same and they are reemphasized.

Always move toward your message points.

Eliminate Complexity

When you are answering reporters' questions, you must eliminate complexity. When dealing with the media, complexity is your enemy. It's not that reporters are stupid (though some are dumb and others are brilliant). It's just that by the time a reporter tries to read hastily written notes days after the interview, they can jumble things up. Even if the reporter doesn't mess-up your words, there is always the chance that the editor, copyeditor or producer will changes things ever so slightly in such a way that your message becomes totally garbled. It is far better to describe one single tree clearly to a reporter than it is to try to explain the entire forest.

Complex answers typically require a reader, listener or viewer to hear your entire answer in order for your comments to make sense. In the real world, this is no problem. But in the media world, where you instantly lose control over your context, you have no guarantee that your audience will have access to your entire answer. In fact, you can be fairly confident that they will only receive a small part of your answer. That's the problem.

When giving a complex answer, there is also a tendency to rebut negative premises and dispense with faulty assumptions before putting forth new, positive ideas. Unfortunately, the media may never pick up on the positive ideas; instead, the focus will be on your rehashing real or imagined problems.

It's not a matter of Keep It Simple Stupid, the old KISS strategy, either. Instead, you should look at it as an intellectual challenge to streamline your answers, getting to the essence of the matter quickly and cleanly. You can't be stupid to do that, and the process isn't necessarily simple. But your answers, devoid of complexity, will be much more likely to reach your intended audience.

Delete Your Database Of Knowledge

When you are entering a media interview, it is sometimes helpful to think of deleting your entire database of knowledge, except for your three main message points. I am only partially kidding!

Many executives get themselves into trouble during an interview because they can't resist the temptation to show off all of their knowledge. When a reporter asks a question, the expert wants to give a 10 minute tutorial on the subject, going deeper and deeper all the while. The corporate executive or spokesperson has now become the reference librarian for the reporter. That's not the role you want to be in. When you give too much information, you lose control over the subject.

Sometimes it is best to think of your brain as being a virtually clean slate when you walk into an interview. The only thing on it should be your three message points. It's not that you should try to sound like a robot, mindlessly repeating your three message points over and over again. It's just that you should focus on your message points, not on displaying all of your knowledge accumulated over the last 20 years.

Of course, you will access your database of knowledge when presented with a question. But you aren't going to go into every detail, nook and cranny of the issue, even though you maybe well versed in these matters. Instead, you will use your knowledge base to provide a short answer that will allow you to seamlessly segue into your message points.

By "deleting" your database of knowledge before you start an interview, you also make the interview process less taxing and stressful. You no longer put pressure on yourself to remember everything you have ever learned about a subject. Instead, you can relax as you provide your answers, confident in knowing that you are headed in the right, preplanned direction.

"I Don't Know" Is A Perfectly Good Answer

It is OK to tell a reporter, "I don't know," but make sure you follow up with, "but I'll find out and get back to you. What is your deadline?" And then make sure you get back to the reporter BY THE DEADLINE. If you can't get hold of the reporter, be sure to cover yourself by emailing or faxing in the answer. If you actually get back to a reporter by the time you said you would, it is extremely unlikely that you will be quoted as saying, "I don't know." However, if you promise to call them with the information and fail to do so, a reporter might quote you as saying, "I don't know."

The media master is never afraid to say, "I don't know," especially to a question to which the answer unknowable. This is because the media master always quickly pivots to another point about which he or she is confident that is closely related to both the question and one of his or her key message points.

When people are afraid to say, "I don't know," they tend to guess an answer. Unfortunately, if you guess wrongly to a reporter, you are not simply guilty of guessing wrongly. You are guilty of being an untrustworthy LIAR. So don't guess.

Obviously, you don't want to answer 10 questions in a row with, "I don't know," but demonstrating that you are not omniscient may actually enhance your reputation.

An Experts Dilemma

There are two types of experts in the world. One type prides himself in being able to think and speak in a logical, rational, linear, detailed, abstract and conceptual manner. This type is often so identified with his logical, rational intellect that he is unable to communicate in any other manner. Accordingly, this expert tends to remain mired in obscurity. While he may have had numerous media interview opportunities, somehow they never turn out quite right. In fact, this expert is rarely quoted, and when he is quoted, he is usually upset that the "stupid reporter picked such a lousy or irrelevant quote." Over time, he seeks out the media less and less, and his media interview opportunities become fewer. He takes comfort in the fact that he never "sold out" like so many other "media whores" in his profession. Our friend is "pure," albeit highly obscure.

Contrast this expert with another kind of expert. She also prides herself in her ability to think and speak in a logical, rational, linear, detailed, abstract and conceptual manner. However, she realizes that her most advanced level of thinking and talking is not appropriate in every circumstance. She understands that the way she talks to her graduate students or her professional colleagues is not the same way she talks to her children, her grandmother, her minister or visitors from another country. She changes her communication style depending on the circumstances.

When she speaks to the news media regarding her area of expertise, she alters her communication style completely. First of all, she avoids abstraction and gives concrete examples. She does not submit to the temptation of using glib generalizations; instead, she gives specific, personal examples to reporters. She is also not too embarrassed to share her excitement and passion for her subject. Finally, she is always on the lookout for real-world examples, especially from pop culture, that are analogous to activities going on in her field, so that she can reference them when talking to the media.

The results? She is interviewed frequently by the media, and she enjoys the intellectual challenge of making her ideas more understandable to a broader audience. She doesn't see it as "talking down"; rather, she sees it as speaking another language to another group of people. She gets good quotes and favorable media coverage, and the more media she does, the more requests come in. This media exposure gives her access to higher and higher level experts within her field, thus increasing her own learning and visibility. Each positive media interaction fuels future developments. Finally, the expert receives nearly universal acclaim, not only from her professional colleagues, but also from the general public. She has followed in the footsteps of Stephen Jay Gould, Daniel Patrick Moynihan and Jane Goodall.

Which expert do you want to be?

Rewrite Questions To Suit You

After you have heard a reporter's question, hold it up to the light and rewrite the question in your own head to make it easier for you to answer it. Note: this is not the same thing as ignoring the question and saying whatever you feel like. The art in this process is finding a way to rewrite the question so it is less threatening to you, while at the same time not appearing to be dodging the question entirely.

For example, a reporter might ask you the following: "How do you feel about the current scandals affecting you and your company, and how this may destroy your career and your company's future prospects?" Seems like a tough question, right? But what if we simply rewrite the question in a simpler fashion, such as, "How do you feel about your prospects for the future?" Answer: "I feel very optimistic about the future because . . ." Now the rewritten question wasn't so hard, was it?

The skill is not in dodging questions or even coming up with brilliant answers. Instead, the more useful skill to have during interviews is the ability to rewrite the questions to make them easier for you to answer. When you rewrite them, you don't want to completely change their meaning. Instead, you want to remove the sting while keeping some of the substance. That way you can substantively address the question without having to get negative or defensive.

So keep rewriting the tough questions until they become easy enough to answer in your own positive terms.

Aim For All Three Message Points – In Every Answer

Of all of the advice I give to my media training clients regarding answering questions in a media interview, the hardest concept for people to grasp is the need to communicate all three of your message points in every answer (that's EVERY answer). When I tell people this, they think that I am kidding, or they think that I meant to say, "All three message points during the course of the interview." That's not what I am saying. I urge people to try to say all three of their message points in every single answer.

"But TJ," they cry. "I'll sound insane! Reporters will run away from me."

No, they won't. The trick is not to sound like a computer or a broken record. You want to hit all three of your message points in each answer, but do it in a different order, using different examples and different words.

If you aim for all three message points and you only get to one or two before the reporter cuts you off or interrupts you, well, then you at least hit one or two – not bad.

The mistake many novices make is that they deliver all three of their message points exactly once, often near the beginning of the interview. Then they proceed to answer questions in a totally reactive way for the next 30 minutes. At the end of the interview, the reporter looks down at his or her notes and sees 57 separate message points, each delivered exactly once – therefore none stand out. The reporter then selects two or three at random these 57 points.

If you are happy with a 3 in 57 chance of success, continue to use this strategy. If you want to increase the odds that the message you care about actually ends up in the story, you must be more proactive, specifically by trying to interject all three of your message points in each answer.

Positive Answers Only

Nothing is more intellectually shallow than a motivational speaker talking about the "Power of Positive Thinking", right? Or, what could be more annoying than local TV anchors doing "happy talk" during the middle of a newscast?

If you pride yourself in being a "straight shooter" or one who "tells it like it is," you are in for a real surprise when dealing with the media. Of course, the news media will appreciate you if you trash your boss, your competitors or especially yourself, but nobody else will. In fact, taking a negative tack is a surefire way to talk yourself out of friends, an employer and even a career.

If you are in the middle of an interview, regardless of what type of questions are being asked, you must try to answer them in positive terms. I'm not advocating telling lies or even sugar-coating them, but how about dipping reality in a small vat of honey before distributing it to the world via the media?

Many people find this challenging because they want to give a "balanced" story, that is, one that conveys both positives and negatives. The problem with attempting to give a balanced story is that only, and I mean ONLY, the negative statements are likely to make it into the final story. For example, if you say, "It's true, my family connections did help me get my first job 25 years ago, but ever since then I've had to work twice as hard to prove that I am not just the son of a celebrity. In fact, I know that blah, blah, blah (more stuff about how hard you worked)," the only quote that is likely to end up in the story is this: "Walker conceded what his critics have always contended, 'It's true, my family connections did help me get my job.'" End of quote.

Remember, a media interview is not a true conversation in which you are rewarded for balance and objectivity. The "balance" in the story will come from the reporter's getting quotes and perspectives from a variety of sources, some of whom may have negative views regarding you and what you do. So if you want to ensure that you are represented in a balanced way, you must be overwhelmingly positive in all of your comments to the news media.

Oh, And One More Thing . . .

It's a temptation that's hard to resist. The interview is over and the reporter asks, "Anything else I forgot to ask?" And you want to say, "Yes, actually there is one more thing . . ."

Don't do it!

If you've gone to the trouble of planning, shaping and delivering a message throughout the course of an interview, this is not the time to abandon that message. Psychological studies show that the strongest impression you make is the first impression, or the first thing you say. But the second strongest impression is the last thing you say. So if you introduce some new and interesting concept at the very end of an interview, there is a good chance that it will land in the story, no matter how many times you stuck to your official message earlier in the interview.

Most smart, ambitious people who are interviewed also pride themselves in being interesting conversationalists. Unfortunately, the structure of a media interview does not allow for this. Nonetheless, these same smart people will toss out the interview rules because they just can't stand the idea that this reporter will think that they are boring hacks. So they will introduce something new at the conclusion of the interview and that becomes the lead in the story. Then for the entire next week at the office, you hear them mumbling and grumbling under their breath, "That #@%$# reporter misquoted me!" Of course, the only fault lies with the interviewee, not the interviewer.

Interview subjects also often make the mistake of thinking the interview is over simply because the reporter has put away the pad and pencil, or the TV camera has been shut off. The interview is never over until the reporter has left your premises or you can hear a dial tone. If you say something interesting while in a reporter's presence, it is fair game for him or her to use it in a story. Unless, you explicitly got the reporter to agree in advance that what you were going to say was off the record.

Jimmy Carter made this blunder in 1976 when he was running for President. He had been interviewed everyday for several weeks by a national magazine reporter. At the end of their time together, the reporter thanked Carter and put away the pad and pencil. Carter then walked the reporter to the door of his home in Plains, Georgia, and said something like, "I just want to stress one thing, yes, I'm a man of faith, and my faith is very important to me. You've seen me teach Sunday school here in Plains. But I'm no better than anyone else. The Bible says if you've even looked at another woman with lust in your heart, that's the same as committing adultery. I've done that. I'm just like everyone else."

A short time later, the headlines in Playboy magazine were, "Jimmy Carter: 'I've committed lust in my heart for other women.'" Carter lost 17 points in the polls the last three weeks of that election, thanks, in part, to this one damaging slip of the tongue in the presences of the press.

So when a reporter asks you if there is anything else you want to add at the end of an interview, the proper response is; "Yes, . . ." and then go on to summarize your three main message points one more time.

Media PresentPro™ Workshop

A two day intensive course that covers all aspects of creating a powerful media message, as well as executing it.

www.mediatrainingworkshop.com

Chapter 6:
Crafting Sound Bites
And Quotable Quotes

The Art Of The Sound Bite

Of all of the elements in the public relations magician's black bag of tricks, none is more mysterious than the crafting of the sound bite, or quote.

The world is divided into two groups: those who instinctively know how to turn any abstract message point into a sound bite and those who don't. For those who know how, it is as easy as breathing or laughing. These people often find themselves in marketing or communications. They have liberal arts degrees and they are creative. For those who don't know how to make something quotable, it's as mysterious as trying to speak in tongues. These people have engineering and business degrees. They are logical, rational, linear thinkers, who view themselves as systematic.

Fortunately, I have created a system that will allow these logical, rational, linear thinkers to turn any message point into a sound bite that is irresistible to even the most hard-bitten journalist. The system is called A BEACH PRO, which is an acronym that stands for analogy, bold action words, emotions, examples, attacks, absolutes, clichés, humor, pop culture references, rhetorical questions and opposition quotes.

Nearly every quote you read in newspapers and trade publications contains one or more of these 11 A BEACH PRO elements. Likewise, nearly every sound bite you see or hear on TV or radio makes use of one or more of them as well. Once you understand that reporters require these structural elements in their stories, it becomes incredibly easy to craft the exact quotes you want.

Reporters need quotes. They are one of the essential building blocks of any good story. Quotes are needed to make the story more interesting, understandable and memorable – thus, reporters also need you!

You should never go into an interview without knowing in advance precisely the exact quotes you want to see in tomorrow's newspaper or tonight's newscast. Note: this is not the same as knowing your general message points; sound bites are much more specific than that.

If you ever go into an interview without knowing what quotes you want to see, you have already failed miserably. And if you are a public relations consultant to an executive who is about to be interviewed, and you haven't supplied the client with specific sound bites, you are guilty of malpractice.

A Beach Pro

Analogy

Bold Action Words
Emotions & Examples
Attacks & Absolutes
Clichés
Humor

Pop Culture References
Rhetorical Questions
Oppositional Quotes

Media Training Worldwide has analyzed direct quotes used in uncountable media sources, and has found all contain one or more of these 11 elements. A BEACH PRO is the memorable acronym given to this set.

Analogies In Your Answers

Reporters love to quote newsmakers using analogies. These figures of speech can be quite useful in taking complicated or abstract concepts and making them more understandable in tangible, visual ways. Often colorful, humorous and opinionated, analogies can also be quite attention grabbing.

"Life is like a box of chocolates. You never know what you'll get inside."
– Forrest Gump

"Men are like a bus; there's always another one coming along."

Part of a journalist's task is to bring new concepts alive for his or her audience. The easiest way to get people to grasp new concepts is to see the similarities to older, already understood concepts. Hence, the beauty of analogies. Reporters, however, are often reluctant to create their own analogies as they may seem to be too opinionated. However, journalists love to quote other people who are using them.

Once you have determined what your message points are, you should then brainstorm to see if there are any analogies associated with your points. If so, be sure to use them in answering a reporter during an interview.

Chances are, your analogies will be quoted.

Use Bold, Action-Oriented Words

Action movies always outsell foreign art films in which people just sit around and talk. All good storytellers (a.k.a. journalists) want to weave action into their tales. So when you are being interviewed, you enhance your chances of being quoted when you use bold, action-oriented words. Here are some examples: destroy, decimated, ripped off, soared, smacked, attack, hugged.

Any word or phrase that suggests bold movement or action is enticing to the reporter's ear. Bold, action-oriented words do not have to be negative or attacking. They can be positive, even loving. Of course, if you promise to "rip his lungs out through his nose," chances are 99 to 1 that you will be quoted. The trick, as always, is to make sure you use action words only if they accurately bring to life your key message points.

Let Your Emotions Flow Freely

Venting your emotions is a surefire way to get quoted by reporters. Journalists are supposed to be unbiased, dispassionate and disinterested. They aren't supposed to show any emotion to their readers, viewers or listeners, for fear of being accused of having bias. However, reporters LOVE quoting newsmakers expressing emotion. Emotion is a part of any great drama, and reporters want their stories to have maximum dramatic impact. So anytime you start a sentence with the following phrases, you are almost guaranteed to see your words, in quotes, make it into the final story:

- "I am outraged that . . ."
- "I am shocked that . . ."

- "It was the happiest day of my life when . . ."
- "We were disappointed that last quarter's results were . . ."
- "I felt sickened by . . ."

Emotions can be powerful devices. Before your put you heart on your sleeve, make sure the emotions you express are completely in sync with the messages you are trying to communicate.

The Quotable Example

One sure way to be quoted by the press is to give specific, tangible examples that demonstrate your message point. Reporters are capable of describing phenomena at the mile-high, abstract level, but if you can give a down-to-earth, real-life example, you increase your chances of being quoted in the story. Reporters can talk about the firearms industry, but they will quote when you talk about your Smith & Wesson revolver. Journalists can write about the market's take on how interest rates will go up, but they will quote you saying, "I'm 100 percent convinced Greenspan will increase interest rates by 0.25 percent."

Abstraction is the enemy of every good journalist. When you can give a clear-cut example to a reporter, it enlivens the story and makes it more understandable to the reader, viewer or listener. That's why you will be quoted when you give examples. Compare:

Statement A: People fled the burning building around midnight.

Statement B: "I awoke to the smell of burning plastic. I threw on my bathrobe and ran down the fire escape."

The second example is a much more vivid statement, and would more likely to be used as a quote.

Many novices at the media game make the mistake of trying to sound "smart" by speaking in an elevated, sophisticated, abstract manner. This counterproductive approach will result in your getting zero quotes, or sound bites, in a story.

To get ahead with the media, always give great examples.

Attack Your Way To The Headlines

The surest way to get quoted by the media is to attack somebody, even if it is yourself. Reporters love attacks. Why? Because attacks are a form of conflict, and every great drama involves conflict.

The best story to cover if you are a reporter is a war. Walter Cronkite became famous by covering World War II. Dan Rather became famous during the Vietnam War. Wars give you a lot to cover, because people are attacking each other every day.

The second best assignment for a reporter is covering a national political campaign. Why? Because the leader of one party is attacking the leader of the other party every single day. And vice versa.

When you attack your opponents, your competitors, your boss or yourself by name, you instantly get reporters excited. The more forceful, pointed or emotional the attack you make, the greater your chances are of being quoted.

"General Electric is destroying the Hudson River!"

"McDonald's is on a mission to make every kid in America weigh 300 pounds."

"I hate myself for forgetting to report all of my campaign contributions."

All of these quotes will make it into final radio, TV and newspaper reports because they contain attacks.

Of course, as always, just because something is interesting to reporters doesn't mean it is a good idea for you to say it. If a part of your message is to attack government waste or inequality, then, by all means, attack away. But never attack anyone or anything in front of a reporter unless you want to see that attack connected with your name in the headlines of tomorrow's paper.

Absolutes Are Absolutely Quote Worthy

Reporters can highlight trends or point out continuing patterns within a news story, but they cannot state things with absolute certainty. However, journalists love to quote newsmakers who state absolutes.

"We will bury you!" – Nikita Khrushchev

"Read my lips. No new taxes!" – George H.W. Bush

Journalists eat up quotes like these from politicians. Absolute phrases are attractive to reporters because they add drama to the story and make a key point more memorable.

Reporters can write or say what happened yesterday and today, or what is expected to happen tomorrow, but a reporter cannot say, "Over my dead body will I sign an executive order mandating his execution." And yet, a reporter will always quote a politician who utters such a phrase.

Stating any message point with strong conviction or finality will increase your odds of getting quoted. Sometimes it can be as simple as interjecting the word "absolutely" into a statement, i.e., "We are absolutely committed to building this bridge by the end of summer."

Additionally, if you use the words "never" or "always," you create an "absolute" quality to your message. Remember, if it is absolutely essential that you get your message quoted in the story, use words that convey an absolute conviction on your part.

Cliché Your Way To The Top

We were all taught to avoid clichés by our high school English teachers, and this is good advice when it comes to writing reports and articles, or even giving speeches. Reporters have also been taught by their instructors to never, ever write or utter clichés in news reports. However, there is one big exception to this rule for both newsmakers and news reporters: reporters LOVE quoting experts, executives and newsmakers using clichés. Why? Because clichés are often a colorful way to make a point. They became clichés in the first place because they were a more memorable way of making a message stick in someone's head.

A journalist's job is to make new information more understandable and more memorable to readers, viewers or listeners. When a reporter combines new information with a cliché that repackages old information, the result is often a more comprehensible, memorable story.

If you want to be a masterful media communicator, sometimes you have to swallow your pride. You have to realize that you are not the journalist or writer – your job is to get your message out. Your high school English teacher might not be impressed if she sees you quoted while using a cliché, but that should not be your concern. Your job is to use quotes that reflect your message.

"At the end of the day . . ."
"The bottom line is . . ."
"We hit a home run when we . . ."

None of these clichés are brilliant, but they may help you insert your main points into a story.

One of my clients was a financial regulator for the State of Florida. His office often had to shut down fraudulent boiler-room operations. His message after each shutdown was that consumers should be cautious if someone calls them at dinner time and offers to turn $5,000 into $10,000 in three weeks in an oil-well investment. That was the message, but how did he get this idea into newspapers, TV and radio?

He said, "Remember, citizens, if it sounds too good to be true, it probably is." Same message as above, but because it is a cliché, the news media quoted him. And they quoted him using this very cliché EVERY TWO MONTHS FOR 20 YEARS.

Not only do clichés work, but they will keep working for you over and over again.

Remember, "If it ain't broke, don't fix it."

Joking Your Way Onto The Airwaves Using Humor

Everybody loves a good laugh or chuckle; reporters are no exception. If you crack a joke or say something humorous in front of a reporter, there is a good chance your quip will end up in the broadcast report or tomorrow's newspaper. Humor is always quotable.

Warning! Humor can be tricky business for the executive communicator. What seems funny among colleagues, friends or a "friendly" journalist at 5:30 p.m. might not seem so funny tomorrow morning when you are reading your comments in the Daily Bugle. Please keep in mind, you can be a highly effective, skilled communicator and never use humor to get your point across through the media.

Sarcasm and teasing types of humor usually don't work well in the media because you lose control of context, and, in the case of print media, you lose the ability to communicate with your voice and facial expressions. Typically, the most effective humor is self-deprecating.

"I refuse to make my opponent's youth and inexperience an issue in this campaign," said Ronald Reagan during the 1984 Presidential debate against Walter Mondale. This was funny and effective because Reagan directed the humor at himself. Nobody thought Mondale was too young or inexperienced, whereas sizeable portions of the public were concerned that Reagan was too old and had seemed "out of it" during the previous debate. Reagan's skillful use of self-deprecating humor defused the age issue during the rest of the campaign.

The problem with using humor in front of the media is that someone, somewhere, is likely to be offended – and now there is a permanent public record of your remarks. For example, a congressman for whom I once worked was unhappy with some renovations being made on the U.S. Capitol. He said, "This couldn't look worse if it were made out of cinder blocks." The comments elicited a few chuckles at the time. But the next day, after the comments were recorded in the local newspapers, his office received an angry letter from the National Association of Cinder Block Manufacturers. "How dare you imply that cinder blocks are anything other than a thing of beauty to behold?" was the gist of their message.

This is why most politicians (and others who appear in the media frequently) appear to be humorless. At some point in their career, they tried out a joke and they were punished by some organized group (and I'm not referring to obviously distasteful jokes that make fun of people on the basis of sex, class, creed or race).

So quip if you must, quip at your own expense and quip at your own risk.

Populate Your Quotes With Pop Culture References

If you want to see your message quoted in the media, one sure way is to add a pop culture reference. Reporter's LOVE anything that relates to someone or something that is currently receiving attention in pop culture or is generally known to the masses.

If you say, "I believe that ACME Company did not make the wisest selection when it hired Dick Smithers to be its new CEO," you are unlikely to be quoted. If you say, "Hiring Dick Smithers to be the CEO is a worse decision than hiring Michael Jackson to be your kid's babysitter," you will be quoted. Reporters aren't going to pass up a reference to Michael Jackson.

A winning Super Bowl quarterback who says, "I'm going on vacation now," won't be quoted. A quarterback who says, "I'm going to Disney World," will be quoted. If you can make an analogy or reference to a current popular movie, film star, famous musician or sports celebrity, you will come as close as you can get to a guaranteed quote from a reporter.

In another example, if you are talking to an information technology trade publication and you want to praise one of your peers in the industry, you are unlikely to be quoted if you use vague and abstract adjectives such as "brilliant" or "resourceful." Instead, if you say, "Dithers is the Tiger Woods of the IT industry," you much more likely to be quoted.

Reporters are looking for words and quotes that will put pictures into the minds of readers, viewers and listeners. Madonna, Michael Jordan, Teddy Roosevelt, Bill Clinton – all of these people instantly create images for people. Institutions can work as well. "I believe Windshield Company is an excellent franchising opportunity" is not quotable. "I believe Windshield Company is going to be the McDonald's of the windshield world" is quotable because everyone has a strong image of McDonald's as a dominant worldwide franchise.

Once you have come up with your message points, brainstorm for pop culture references that can dramatize your message; you will be much more likely to see your quotes make the final story.

Comment With A Rhetorical Question

One great way to get your message quoted by reporters is to state your ideas in the form of a rhetorical question. Why do reporters like rhetorical questions? Because journalists like to break up the structure of their stories. If every sentence begins with a subject followed by a verb and ends with an object, the story gets boring very quickly. An occasional rhetorical question surrounded by quotation marks helps mix up the flow of a story.

"Are you better off today than you were four years ago?"

"Are we going to face a possible bankruptcy next year?"

"When is management going to listen to its own workers?"

"When will the airline unions realize that if they get all of their demands, there will be no airlines left in business?"

"Why has the governor betrayed the faith of the voters?"

"Will Microsoft Office revolutionize the way workers get their jobs done?"

The one thing all of these questions have in common is that they aren't real questions. They aren't expressions uttered by someone seeking new information. They are rhetorical questions, meaning they are simply a way of making a point in the form of asking a question; the question doesn't have to be answered in order for the point to be made.

Do I think it's good to communicate your message points in the middle of an interview by using rhetorical questions? Yes, I do.

Opposition Quotes

Another effective way to get your message quoted is for you to quote someone or something that is opposing you or providing a contrast to your viewpoint.

"My opponent, our current governor, said, 'Elect me and I'll create one million new jobs.' But what he didn't tell us at the time is that he would create those jobs in China!"

That is an opposition quote. You are putting words into the mouth of someone else and then responding to them. This sound-bite element is often used in an attack, for obvious reasons.

At least once a month, I see some major celebrity who is going through an expensive divorce quoted this way: "As Shakespeare once said, 'The first thing we should do is kill all the lawyers.'" It's not original (and lawyers can make the case that the quote is taken out of context), but the quote is irresistible to most reporters.

Opposition quotes can often be complex, and they usually rely on some explicit or implicit attack, therefore they aren't appropriate for most corporate executives. However, opposition quotes remain a favorite of reporters, so use them only if and when they truly help convey your message.

Recycling Can Be Environmentally
And Rhetorically Correct

Many people say to themselves, "I'm just not good at being creative, clever or fast on my feet during media interviews. That's why my interviews are often hit or miss."

Fortunately, being successful with the media does not require being fast or clever on your feet during the middle of an interview, although that can be an asset. Many skillful media communicators understand that getting their message out and receiving the exact quotes they want has nothing to do with creativity or spur-of-the-moment thinking. Instead, it involves giving the media information that is prepackaged in a format that satisfies their basic needs.

One of my first real jobs out of college was serving as director of communications for the Florida Department of Banking and Finance, which was headed by a statewide-elected official, the Florida comptroller, Gerald Lewis. One of the responsibilities of the office was to shut down illegal, fraudulent investment companies running boiler-room operations that were common in South Florida in the 1980s.

In consulting with the legal staff, Lewis came up with the following message intended for Florida citizens (not to mention voters!): "If someone calls you during the dinner hour soliciting $5,000 from you to invest in an oil well, and they claim to be able to double your money in 90 days, and yet you don't know this person or have any connection to the firm, there is a good chance that you may be the victim of a fraudulent securities offering." That was the message and it was an important message. But would the media print that verbatim in the newspaper or use a sound bite like that on the 6 p.m. news? Of course not.

Instead, Lewis packaged his message into a more media-friendly manner by using a cliché. So at every press conference he said the following: "Remember, citizens, if it sounds too good to be true, it probably is." That was it, just a simple, old cliché. Nothing funny, original or creative. And what were the results? Always the same. Lewis got the exact quote he wanted expressing the precise message he wanted in newspapers, radio and television news every two months FOR THE 20 YEARS HE WAS IN OFFICE.

Lewis understood correctly that communicating through the media is not about impressing your high school English teacher; it is about one thing only: getting your message out so that it is actually received and understood by your intended audience. So when you have a quote or sound bite that has worked for you in the past, recycle it – use it again and again. You aren't being judged on your creativity. You are being graded on whether you got your message out.

(I know that I recycled this story from another one I wrote just a few pages ago. While this is annoying in a book that is read in a straightforward manner, it is effective as a media strategy.)

The Limits Of Spin

Every once in awhile you see a politician get in such a pickle that you realize there is no media message that could possibly help him or her spin his or her way to safety. For example, Jack Ryan, a Republican candidate for the U.S. Senate from Illinois, found himself in just such a situation.

Ryan had won the nomination for the Republican Party, i.e., the political party that has spent fortunes reminding voters for the last three decades that it is the party of "traditional values" such as no extramarital sex (unlike certain Presidents!), no gay sex and no sex of any kind that would not be approved of on an I Love Lucy bedroom set. Trouble is, though, Ryan's ex-wife swore under oath that he repeatedly took her to sex clubs in hot spots around the globe and tried to pressure her into having sex with him in front of total strangers.

Oops!

This is more than a little embarrassing. So how did Ryan try to spin his way out of this?

He reminded people that "he broke no laws." Interesting, but no one accused him of breaking laws. He claimed, "I didn't lie under oath." Nice, but no one accused Ryan of perjury. Ryan whined that all he did was "proposition my own wife." Well, that's one way of looking at it. Nothing Ryan said seemed to satisfy the media or any of his supporters. All of his contributors and party leaders ran away from him so quickly that his campaign simply collapsed.

Ryan failed to understand that what everyone wanted to know was how he could try to be a representative of the Traditional "No Sex" Political Party while at the same time having, shall we say, "modern" views on the appropriateness of having sex in public (with a movie star wife, no less).

There is hypocrisy and then there is HYPOCRISY. It's one thing to be against outsourcing and caught wearing a tie made in China; it's another to be Dean Martin with a martini in hand running for President of the Temperance League.

It's one thing if scandal hits you once you are already in office, but if you are a candidate like Ryan, you have no institutional support to sustain you in tough times. I don't see how he could have survived, short of paying his former wife to admit she'd lied under oath (something most ex-wives are reluctant to do).

But, some of you must be thinking, didn't Bill Clinton weather a similar storm with Jennifer Flowers during the 1992 presidential campaign? The difference is that Clinton was not a member of the No Sex Party. For Clinton, a similar campaign-threatening event would have been if he had secretly owned slaves in the mid-'80s and used the N-word. That would have cut him down in a way that even he could not have spun his way out of.

So remember, as great as good spin can be, it can't get you out of every jam.

Chapter 7:
Social Media

Should I do video blogging?

Yes.

Anything you do in a text format, you should also do in a video format. You don't have to hire Spielberg or Lucas to direct; just talk to a webcam and put out your ideas.

The phrase "video blog" means a lot of different things to different people, in the same way blogging means different things too. I am using the phrase here to mean any video you create yourself and put up on the web that is not a part of some huge, traditional media company like ABC or NBC. So video blogging could mean trivial reflections on what you had for breakfast, but it could also mean doing slick, highly produced hour-long training videos.

Video blogs can come in many different forms. Here are ten big categories:

1. Video reflections of a personal and/PR professional nature, similar to anything you might currently write in a blog now.
2. Video press releases where you simply restate the facts of your press release.
3. Commentary on top news stories of the day. This is what I do every day on my video blog and on YouTube.
4. Pitch videos where you send producers your best sound bites on a subject in the hopes that they book you on their show.

5. Re-purposing media videos, i.e. if you are on CNBC or the Today Show, showcase your video in a place where everyone can see it.
6. Re-purpose your speeches. If you give a speech, why not video record the whole thing and then release the whole video or edit it into interesting chunks and put on your video blog.
7. How-to videos; present straight forward information on evergreen topics in a simple talking head video format. (I release these every day too, though some are recycled.)
8. Produced video segments. If you have the time and inclination, create a traditionally produced and edited video on a subject matter of importance to you and make it look as if it could be on the evening network news or even 60 Minutes.
9. Endorsement videos. Video can be a great way to give a reference for an employee or vendor. Testimonial videos for friends, colleagues and associates can be easier and faster than text version and can have much more impact and lasting impression.
10. The so-called "viral video." This is mentioned last because it is the hardest to do and is highly confusing to people. But if you have a concept for a video that is outrageously funny or wildly provocative, then you should perhaps spend the time to produce it with the intention of making something that people will pass along, thus helping you reach a large audience.

I personally use all ten versions of video blogging options myself. Also, you will find there are sub-versions for many of these categories. For example, instead of creating a pitch video for the news media I might create what I call a supplement media video. In this case, a reporter has called me up to interview me in a particular subject, say, how a politician did in a major debate or campaign speech. I set up a mutually agreed time to do the interview in one hour. Next, I quickly formulate my thoughts on the topic. Then, I shoot a quick 90 second video where I dump all of my thoughts in a concise, sound bite fashion. Next, I email the video to the reporter. I still do the interview as planned at the scheduled time. But I tell the reporter that I have created a video just for him or her and it can be used exclusively for the online version of their story. Now, instead of getting just a couple of quotes, I get twice as many quotes because the reporter can pull more out of the video AND I get the video attached as a link (often with a large thumbnail photo) on the web page where the story is located. This can't be guaranteed every time, but it does happen and it's a simple thing to try.

Over time, you will come up with your own uses for your video blog. There are few hard and fast rules except for this—if you can do it in text, you should likely be doing it in video format as well.

How long should an Internet video be?

As long as it takes, is the short answer, but it is more complicated than that. Some Internet sensations like Gary Vaernerchuck of TV Wine library does videos of 10-30 minutes of lengths—long by conventional Internet standards. And yet he is widely viewed and wildly successful. And there are millions of 30 second videos on YouTube that have 5 views or fewer. So being short isn't the answer to everything.

When you are planning a YouTube video, your first concern should not be the length of the video. Your primary concern should be having an interesting message that other people will find relevant, useful, entertaining or enlightening. If you focus on that, length will usually take care of itself.

However, there are a few things to take into consideration. At the moment, many people do prefer quick bites of video at a morning or lunch time break. So why give them a half an hour video if you know they will stop after 3 minutes?

The rule of thumb I try to follow when creating internet videos is this: stick to one idea, one topic and one main point, and say it as briefly as possible without leaving out all of your good stuff. Personally, I find than most of my daily news commentary videos are between 60 to 90 seconds with some occasionally going to two or even three minutes.

Also remember that you don't have to aim for an exact, precise time like 30 or 60 seconds. Those exact times mattered in traditional linear broadcast venues where everything is scheduled and programmed around a set grid. But social media and internet video isn't like that, so take a little more time or a little less time if that's what you need. If you've got a great message, you might be able to say everything you need to in 9 seconds. But if you've produced a world-class documentary that's 3 hours long, you might be able to get a huge internet audience for that too.

Another option is to break up our videos into part 1, part 2, etc. This way people can take bite sizes without ever feeling impatient. There is a certain psychology involved with your viewers. If you make your videos consistently interesting and consistently short, then you always are leaving them wanting more. However, if your viewers are consistently jumping out of your videos before they finish, you are conditioning them to turn you off and to make judgments that you may be boring them. All things being equal, it's better not to do that, so err on the side of being just long enough to be really interesting and not one second longer.

Like a lot of things on the internet and with new media, the answer to how long your video should be is "it just depends." I realize that sounds wishy washy, but it is a reality.

What kind of camera should I use?

Frankly? It doesn't matter. Sure, all things being equal, use the highest quality camera you can find. But most people waste way too much time trying to figure out the best camera. Instead, they should focus on creating as much interesting and compelling talking head videos as possible.

Personally, I use the built in webcam on my $400 laptop quite frequently. I also use my $150 Flip camera, or my cell phone. Occasionally, I will use the video capabilities on my digital still photography camera too.

Your cameras matter a great deal when you are shooting a movie and people are going to be seeing your face 60 feet high or for an ad on the Superbowl. But when it comes to creating simple talking-head videos for use in social media, I recommend that you have a variety of inexpensive cameras and use whatever is flexible and easy on a daily basis.

Think of it the same way you create email. Few people ask "what is the best tool for creating email?" That's because when you are at home you probably have a home computer to write email. Then when you are in a cab, bus or car, you are sending email from your phone. At the office you might be sending email from your desktop. Similarly with internet video, use what is easy, simple, fast and convenient.

In my office, I have a couple of consumer grade HD video cameras set up in front of my backdrop so I can walk in at anytime and tape breaking news commentary. When I am at home, I often use my laptop's webcam. When I am on a train or cab and in a big hurry, I will use a Flip. Guess what, for the most party, no one cares. People care about my ideas and they judge me on those, as long as the audio is clear and they can see my face.

How you look is important when it comes to video, but don't fall into the trap of obsessing over the technology. Sure some technology is better than others. But most individuals and businesses that really succeed promoting themselves through internet social media do so because they convey interesting ideas with passion, not because they have the latest and best camera.

If you are on a budge, and who isn't these days, also realize that if people are watching you on small computer screens ,then the magic and beauty of $50,000 cameras won't be very apparent. That's why I typically use inexpensive consumer grade cameras rather than broadcast quality cameras, even though I have both. If you want to save money, then buy an inexpensive HD consumer grade camera and then make sure you have a decent light or two and a good microphone. For a simple talking head social media video, ample light, a decent mic, and having the camera at an angle so that it doesn't look like it is shooting up your nose is all you need to come across professionally and competently.

What do I do if a print reporter pulls out a flip video camera and wants to record the video for his website?

You say "yes!" and you do a little dance of joy!

If a reporter is doing a text-based story on you and is now willing to do a video interview with you, this means you are getting a two-for-one special-- that's nice at the local Wal-Mart and in your PR campaign as well.

If a newspaper columnist or internet reporter, or even a radio reporter wants to do a video interview with you while using a Flip or other small hand-held video camera, please keep these concepts in mind:

1. Video is video whether you are on NBC's Today Show in high definition or if you are on an obscure trade publications website. Sure the number of eye balls may differ but you can either look conformable, confident and relaxed or nervous, uncomfortable, and rumpled in either case.

2. Look at yourself in a mirror before doing the interview to make sure your hair is combed, you have no spinach in your teeth and that your tie and/or jacket, blouses is straight.

3. Don't' look at the camera unless the reporter asks you to. Instead, just look at the reporter when you are speaking.

4. Ask the reporter how long a segment he or she would like to go for. Try to make your answers fit the time length so that the reporter doesn't have to edit the video.

5. Never ask the reporter to edit out something you say or your uhs and ums. Assume everything is live-to-tape. This means you will save the reporter lots of time and effort by not having to edit.

6. Assume the camera is still recording even when the reporter says the interview is over—you never know!

7. Ask the reporter to send you the URL of the video link and offer to promote the link to all of your professional contacts via Facebook, Twitter and all other social media connections you have—reporters will appreciate this.

Also, keep in mind the following 10 tips that apply to regular TV interviews also apply to Internet Flip video interviews:

1. Lean forward 15 degrees toward the camera.
2. Move your head.
3. Move your hands.
4. Move your body.
5. Wear solids (but not black, white or bright red)
6. Speak slightly louder than usual.
7. Speak with more energy than usual.
8. Focus on just three message points.
9. Have a few sound bites prepared for each message point.
10. Be conversational

Remember, the internet may create new kinds of media, social media and other outlets for communication, but some things will never change: if you have interesting messages and can communicate them in an engaging, confident and lively manner, you will do fine no matter what new gizmos are deployed by information gatherers.

Chapter 8:
Honing Your Skills

You Can Be A Star Without Having Star Talent

One of the most exciting things to me about learning to give good presentations or interviews is that, unlike becoming a great actor, basketball player or singer, it doesn't take any innate skill. Anyone who really tries can become a very good, if not an excellent, speaker. All it requires is a little work, practice and the willingness to show up. No matter how many golf lessons I take or how many rounds off golf I practice, I can assure you that no one will ever pay me money to watch me play golf. Fortunately, the same is not true for me or most people when it comes to speaking.

Millions of people may signup to audition for a chance to sing on American Idol, but how many people in your office signup for a chance to give a presentation to your board of directors? This is the great reality about speaking and presenting: most people will do anything to avoid it. Therefore, it is easy to distinguish yourself in an activity that no one wants to participate in, whereas it is hard to distinguish yourself in an area like singing, because everyone wants to do it.

I learned at an early age that when it comes to giving a speech, good things happen to people simply for showing up. The sheer act of making a public presentation or stepping in front of the camera can distinguish you from your colleagues, even if you aren't an outstanding speaker yet.

When I was 12 years old and about to graduate from the sixth grade, my teacher, Mrs. Stroup, was in charge of putting on the graduation ceremony for the parents, teachers and students. She was in a quandary; she couldn't find a student to give the welcoming speech to the assembly. She approached me in a slightly flustered state and said, "TJ, how would you like to make a deal?"

I said, "What?"

She said, "Right now you have A's in all of your courses but a C in handwriting. How would you like to make an A in handwriting?"

I responded, "Sure!"

Thus, a deal was struck. I would deliver the welcoming speech to the graduation ceremony. I wish I could tell you I was a child prodigy and that I had the audience cheering and delivering a standing ovation. Instead, I said something like, "Parents, teachers and fellow students, welcome to the Bruns Avenue Elementary School Sixth Grade Graduation Ceremony. Thanks for coming." And then I sat down!

I wasn't the Mozart of the speaking world, but I did learn an important lesson: if you are willing to stand up and speak, especially in front of large crowds, people will reward you!

More Is More In Media World

Nothing screams out "amateur hour" more than a self-important business executive who tells his public relations consultants the following: "I don't want to do talk radio or local TV or just be quoted in stories about other companies or trends. I just want profile stories about me and my company in major business publications like The Wall Street Journal or Fortune." My advice to anyone who is this narrow in thinking is to simply buy advertising. Public relations through media exposure requires a long-term commitment if you want to see results; it can't be done with a snap of the finger in short, episodic bursts.

The first question you have to ask yourself is, "Can I benefit by becoming well known to my universe of relevant people via the media?" If the answer is yes, then you need to work on making yourself extraordinarily interesting, quotable and available to your target media. If all you care about is people in the concrete industry, perhaps you have to target only half a dozen trade publications and newsletters in the concrete industry, but target them like crazy. Make yourself available for interviews. Make sure key editors and reporters have your home phone and cell phone numbers. Ask to write guest columns. Write letters to the editor. Dominate your space.

If you wish to become well known by the business community at large or the general news-consuming audience, you have to spread a much wider net. You need to be omnipresent. Unless you are Janet Jackson or Jennifer Lopez, the threat of overexposure is minimal. There are roughly 12 billion media outlets in the world today; it is nearly impossible for anyone except for a small group of entertainment celebrities to become overexposed. The real problem that 99.99999 percent of the rest of us have is underexposure.

That's why our books don't get onto the bestseller list. That's why our software doesn't sell five million units.

Yes, being selective and discerning can be great qualities to have in terms of distinguishing your career, but these rules don't apply when it comes to advancing your way up the media food chain. Turning down a talk-radio phone interview on a small station in Spokane, Washington, may seem like a no-risk way for you to save 15 extra minutes in your day. But there are hidden losses, too. Appearing as a guest on a small station for 15 minutes is a chance for you to hone your act as an interesting expert guest. You shouldn't pass up the chance for this experience; even famous Broadway actors open a show in Hartford before exposing themselves to New York City critics.

Next, if you do generate interest from NBC Radio or National Public Radio bookers or producers, they may ask you what other radio shows you've been on lately. If the answer is "None," they might decide you are too "green" to go on the national airwaves. The fact that you have done a small local radio appearance is an insurance policy for the national media.

Finally, you can never underestimate how quickly people change their jobs in the media business. A 23-year old talk-radio producer for a news-radio station in Des Moines, Iowa, could easily be a booker for MSNBC or the Fox News Channel only two weeks after you appeared as a guest on the small-town station. If you turn down the first interview in Iowa, you won't be in the producer's Rolodex two weeks later when he or she is scrambling around to find a panelist on national TV. You've just blown your opportunity for major national exposure.

Many of the people who get the most publicity in the highest prestige media are also the same folks who will appear on the most obscure talk-radio show or who will allow themselves to be interviewed by a college newspaper. They don't waste time analyzing and fretting about whether the audience or readership is big enough or prestigious enough. They just do it.

Look at renowned attorney Alan Dershowitz of Harvard Law School. Yes, he gets in the New York Times frequently, and he is a regular on ABC's Nightline, but he is seen and heard in many other places, too. Sure, he is smart and articulate, but so are a lot of law professors. Dershowitz gets regular access to prestigious media because he is extremely accessible to ALL media. He gives out his cell phone number freely to any journalist. He doesn't mind doing short spots on cable TV news during off hours when few people are watching. He's happy to talk about any legal issue, even when it has nothing to do with the current book he is promoting. If you are a talk-radio booker in Sioux Falls, South Dakota, you might not be able to book a local law professor for a 15-minute legal debate, but you can sure get Dershowitz. Heck, you could be a talk-show host on a junior high school radio station heard by 10 other students, and you would probably be able to get Dershowitz to be a guest on your show – maybe not for two hours, but at least for five minutes.

How does all of this time and hard work benefit Dershowitz? If he writes a great book (as I think he does from time to time), he is assured that that book will make it onto the New York Times bestseller list, thus creating another small fortune. If he slaps together a lousy book that consists of nothing but some old columns stapled together (which I also think he does from time to time), that book is also guaranteed a spot on the bestseller list because of all of the name recognition he has. Because of his media exposure, Dershowitz can also charge more for a one-hour speech than many Americans make in a full year. His fame allows him to charge legal clients incredibly high fees as well.

You might not like Dershowitz's politics or style, but those are not the point. Ultimately, it's not about your politics or even the size of your ego. Instead, it's about this: can you communicate your message to the widest possible group of people in your target audience and can you do it regularly?

Just as the actor creed states there are no small parts, only small actors, for the public communicator, there are no insignificant media opportunities, only insignificant communicators.

The X-Factor: Fun

I am often asked, "What is the difference between a good communicator and a great communicator?" In professional golf, the difference between someone who makes a fortune on the tour and someone who struggles to pay his caddy is, on average, only one or two stroke. Similarly, for those who give speeches or communicate on TV, the difference between the good and the great is very small. In fact, the "good" presenters often make fewer mistakes, stumble less or jump around less frequently. The "great" speakers often make all of these blunders and more, yet they still come off as fantastic and memorable communicators.

Why?

The difference all comes down to fun. Fantastic communicators are having fun when they communicate. They show it in their face, their eyes, their voice, their hands and their body language. Great speakers consistently communicate the following: "There is no place on Earth I'd rather be than speaking in front of you right now or appearing on this TV show to talk about what it is that I do."

Audiences also respond very well to a speaker's genuine passion. That doesn't mean that in order to be a good speaker you have to jump up and down like a televangelist or sound full of hype like that kid on the infomercials hawking a get-rich-quick scheme involving selling stuff through "tiny, tiny classified ads" if only you will first send him $245.

There is no one way to prove that a speaker is having a lot of fun when talking about a subject, but, like Justice Potter Stewart, who couldn't define pornography but knew it when he saw it, live audiences and TV audiences instantly feel when a presenter is having fun. Audiences might not know why, but they feel it in their bones.

The next question I get is, "TJ, how in the heck can I have fun when I'm nervous, and I'd rather be having heart surgery – without anesthesia – than be giving a speech or appearing on TV?" Sadly, I have no simple magic answer for you. Betty Buckley is a star Broadway performer in part because she has practiced daily for decades. Even the 14-year-old prodigies who occasionally spring up in women's tennis, golf and ice skating didn't become great over night. They practiced for hours a day for a decade before they went pro.

Fortunately, you don't have to give speeches for hours a day to become great, but you do have to give them often enough so that you are no longer excessively nervous. Then, and only then, can you focus on the joy of communicating on your subject of choice.

Learn From Friend And Foe Alike

One thing that separates good communicators from great communicators is that the great ones are constantly on the prowl for new ideas on how to improve their style, technique and delivery process – and they don't care where they get these ideas. With an eye for both style and substance, great communicators can listen to other speakers and judge them simultaneously on content and form.

Most people don't do this. The average person listens to or watches a speaker and judges only from the perspective of content. What was the message? At a less than fully conscious level, most of us judge whether we like someone and if they make us feel comfortable, but that's as far as it goes. If we don't like someone's message, we tend to dismiss him or her as a bad person or someone not worthy of our attention.

The result?

Liberal Democrats don't listen to Rush Limbaugh and refuse to learn anything about his communication strengths because they don't like his conservative message. Conservative Republicans can't watch Bill Clinton on a TV screen for more than 20 seconds without shouting at the screen and turning the channel because they don't like him personally. Many moderates turn off anyone they perceive as having strong opinions of any persuasion. All three groups are missing out on tremendous learning opportunities.

Master communicators watch and listen to the widest array of speakers, politicians and commentators. They then borrow, mix and match the best practices of others to use in their own future speeches.

The liberal master communicator will listen to Rush Limbaugh for hours and marvel at his skill for maintaining a conversational tone of voice, sounding spontaneous and interjecting humor and sheer cleverness into his presentation. The liberal pro learns from
Limbaugh and doesn't turn him off the second he utters a disagreeable opinion.

The conservative master communicator will watch Bill Clinton speak for hours whenever the opportunity presents itself. The conservative pro revels in Clinton's mastery of eye contact, his ability to project warmth and empathy, and his dazzling articulateness, which allows him to speak in flawlessly constructed sentences and paragraphs for long periods of time. The conservative communicator pro doesn't tune out Clinton just because of a distaste for his personality.

It's not that high-level communicators should imitate every other great speaker they see – the goal is not to mimic or be an impersonator. But by regularly making yourself aware of how other people communicate well, you become more aware of your own strengths and the areas in which you need to improve. Master communicators may add a new element to their presentation style gradually, but they never make wholesale changes to the way they speak or simply imitate a famous speaker.

If you want to become a great communicator, you must develop the practice of using both of your ears at the same time for different purposes. Use your left ear to hear the content and the message. And use your right ear (and eyes) to identify the style, technique and form of the speaker to whom you are listening. This way you will learn from every speaker you encounter – even if it is learning what NOT to do.

Break the Rules, But First Learn Them

In every discipline, there are a few masters who seemingly break all of the rules yet still excel. Tennis sensation Björn Borg started off on the wrong foot, but he still conquered Wimbledon numerous times. Orson Welles never bothered with film school, yet Citizen Kane was a great success.

Similarly, there are the rule breakers in the world of media. One of the things I teach my clients is to sit-up high and lean forward 15 degrees into the camera when appearing on TV. This makes most people look taller, thinner and more dynamic, while accentuating their jaw line – traits most people desire. If you sit back in your chair and relax on TV, you will tend to look short, fat, bored and sloppy. As a general rule, the 15-degrees-forward posture will enhance your image and increase the chances that you don't distract viewers from your message.

But . . . is it as ironclad a rule as the law of gravity?

No. For 35 years, as the host of PBS's Firing Line, William F. Buckley sat way back in his chair in a semi-reclined position. He broke the rules and yet his TV-commentary career flourished.

So is the rule of leaning forward invalidated?

No. Buckley simply flourished because he had so many other strengths in place: a sharp wit, an inclination to attack, a distinctive style and a willingness to be one of the only conservatives addressing the mainstream media in the '60s (this was the pre-Limbaugh, Fox News, talk-radio era).

I urge my clients to learn the fundamentals of speaking well in front of audiences and TV cameras before experimenting with breaking the rules. If you are already famous, as was Buckley before he began his TV career, you have more leeway in establishing a TV persona. If you are currently a non-famous corporate spokesperson or author, you run the risk that your idiosyncrasies will distract audiences from your central message. That's why I urge clients not to wear loud clothing, big jewelry or wacky makeup when appearing on TV, even if that is their normal or trademarked appearance. TV is such a visual medium that unusual visuals will crowd out your message.

I'm not suggesting that you have to be bland and boring and dress like every news anchorman from Cleveland, but if you are trying to communicate your ideas to the public via the mass media, it is far better to have your message dominate rather than your appearance. Once you have established a firm public identity, then you may wish to experiment with breaking the rules. But beware of losing control over your message.

Parlay Your Prominence

"On this date in history, 200 years ago today, Patrick Henry said . . ."

These were the first words I ever spoke on television. It was the fall of 1975, and I was selected to do a "Bicentennial Minute" as part of the United States' celebration of its upcoming 200th   birthday. No, I wasn't on the CBS network or even the local NBC affiliate. Instead, my TV/media career began on a closed-circuit TV newscast of the Quail Hollow Junior High School in Charlotte, North Carolina. (Total audience: 1,200 students, 75 teachers.)

I was the mini-celebrity of the school hallways for the entire next day! Thus began my lifelong fascination with the media. I was a mere seventh grader at the time, the lowest of the low in a junior high school pecking order. How did I get selected for school-wide TV exposure?

I wish I could say it was due to winning an international science project or convincing the City Council to create a new park, but the truth is, I had won a Fonzie look-alike contest the day before at an after-school '50s-day sock hop. With a too tight T-shirt, pair of jeans and greased-back hair, I let out a few "Heyssss" the way the '70s sitcom character Fonzie did, and I was proclaimed king of the sock hop.

Part of my reward was getting to deliver the history segment of the school newscast the next day. Did this instantly catapult me to the top echelon of cool kids, dates with cheerleaders, etc.? Not exactly. But it did help me get name recognition enough to get elected to the student council a few months later, and that was the first step toward getting elected student body president a year and a half later.

You may be asking yourself, "What in the heck does looking like a stupid sitcom character have to do with being qualified for office, any office, even one as inconsequential as student council? Isn't this what's wrong with our culture today?" And you would be right. In fact, there is no relevance.

However, in a microcosmic way this mirrors how the media world intersects with the real world all the time. If you gain prominence in one field, you can often instantly get media attention that can give you prominence in another unrelated field.

What does being a beauty queen have to do with being a hardnosed journalist? Nothing, but ABC's Diane Sawyer was able to parlay her tenure as America's Junior Miss into the top tier of TV journalism.

What does knowledge of boxing have to do with being a great psychologist? Nothing, but Dr. Joyce Brothers was able to milk her 1955 victory appearance on The $64,000 Question game-show (her topic: boxing) into becoming the country's top pop psychologist for decades.

What does running around in your shorts, sweating and playing with a ball have to do with making sound public policy that affects the lives of a nation? Again, nothing. But Bill Bradley, the former New York Knicks basketball player was able to use his media exposure to hop right into the U.S. Senate at the tender age of 35 without ever having served a day in lesser office. (Yes, he had been a Rhodes Scholar, but there have been hundreds of Rhodes Scholars who haven't gotten elected to anything.)

The point is this: when planning your career, sometimes you have to take an indirect route. If you are good at one thing at one stage in your life, you may want to milk it for all it's worth to get as much media attention as possible, because whatever media attention you get now can help you immensely in whatever the next stage of your career may be.

Chapter 8:
Learning Do's (And One Don't) From Media Figures

Paul Harvey...................Good Day!

The aspiring great communicator should always be on the lookout for good role models. One of the best you could ever find is on a radio dial near you – national news commentator Paul Harvey. Harvey has been broadcasting daily, since, roughly, 1890. He's now approximately 157 years old. Yet he sounds the same as he did 10, 20, even 40 years ago. (If you have never heard of Paul Harvey, try to find the #1-rated news/talk AM radio station in your town. Harvey does four news/comment/feature segments of varying lengths daily.)

Harvey is an absolute master at using the full range of his voice and the pause to their maximum advantage. (It's quite an advantage – he makes tens of millions of dollars a year!) Harvey always has perfect delivery: he sounds conversational, and his voice ranges high, low and everything in between. If he's amused, his voice registers amusement. When he finds something contemptuous, you hear it instantly in his voice. You can pull a 60-second excerpt from any part of Harvey's broadcast and feel like you are on a roller coaster – the ups and downs in his voice never sound contrived, and they always make you feel as though you have embarked on an interesting journey.

Try listening to a five-minute segment from Harvey and contrast that with a five-minute segment from a typical businessperson's speech. (It will not be a pretty comparison.) You will notice several differences. The average businessperson will get about twice as many words out during those five minutes as Harvey does. But, and this is an important but, you will find that an hour later, you will remember nothing from the businessperson's speech and many things from Harvey's broadcast.

In addition to using the entire range of his voice for maximum expressive effect, Harvey is also the master of doing nothing. That's right, nothing, i.e., pausing after talking. Harvey knows that the way to emphasize something is to pause. The way to build drama is to pause. The way to build anticipation is to pause. The way to get your audience to visualize is to pause. The way to get your audience to reflect is to pause. The way to sound 1,000 times more comfortable, confident and relaxed than everyone else when speaking to a large audience is to pause.

Harvey even has a signature pause in his closing. According to him, early in his career he simply ran out of enough material for a tightly timed broadcast segment. He finished his script, then said nothing for several seconds and then concluded with, "Good day!" Somehow it worked and when he realized it worked, he kept doing it. Now tens of thousands of broadcasts later, Harvey ends his commentaries with the signature, "Paul Harvey . . . (pause for several seconds) . . . Good day!"

One Size Fits All

One commonly held mistaken notion about TV personalities is that they have an on-screen persona and an off-screen persona. True, there are some hyperbolic, screaming talking heads, like exercise guru Tony Little, who are actually quiet and mild-mannered in real life. However, most skilled TV communicators appear exactly the same in real life, one-on-one, as they do on the tube.

As a 10-year-old in the early '70s, I started watching an inordinate amount of news and public affairs programming, including William F. Buckley's Firing Line on PBS. As an aspiring pundit myself, Buckley's multifaceted media career was an inspiration, even though I didn't necessarily follow his brand of politics. Of course, Buckley broke many generic rules about television, including how to sit, and he clearly ignored the one about not using big, big words that you know most of your audience will not understand.

However, Buckley did have some major strengths as a communicator, namely, the following: a zest for debate, cheeriness, a sense of fun, quick-wittedness and an appreciation for an intellectual argument, even when it was not his own. Buckley was rarely flustered. He seemed to enjoy the role he had cast for himself: Hollywood's version of the aristocratic, patrician, old-world, faux-European intellectual. Buckley had a way of saying, "Please pass the salt," with a tone in his voice that suggested, "Close the gate before the unwashed rabble overtake our castle and commit acts of unspeakable barbarism." And yet he seemed likable, albeit in an extraordinarily elitist sort of way.

So was it all an act? Was he really a down-home, beer-swilling, Yogi Berra – quoting populist in real life?

Once I was boarding a plane from Chicago on my way back to New York City. There, sitting in first class, was Mr. Buckley. Unfortunately, I was plodding back to economy class. My chances at a mini-debate were dashed.

Back at LaGuardia Airport in New York, I was standing at the baggage reception area waiting for my TV cameras and other luggage and there was Mr. Buckley, standing alone. Now was my chance.

Should I try to be clever: "Did you lose your limo driver?" (Buckley wrote a famous book called Overdrive, which gave exquisite details about his limousine and its driver, creating much envy in most people who read the book.)

No, that wouldn't do.

Should I be polemical? "Can you defend your colleague Pat Buchanan's anti-semitism in light of . . . ?"

No, that wouldn't do either.

Instead, I offered a friendly, "Hello, Mr. Buckley. We miss Firing Line. Any chance of taping some specials?"

He looked at me, smiled, and said, "Ah, yes, Firing Line. I gave that up for the millennium. Thirty-five years was a good run."

He looked the same as he did on TV. He sounded the same. His tongue darted out of his mouth the same. And he even managed to slip in a word that I can't spell (without the help of spell-check) in less than six seconds of conversation.

Buckley, the TV guy, is exactly the same as Buckley in real life.

There is a consistency for which any good communicator should strive, even if your style is completely different from Buckley's. When you find something that works for you, don't change it. Too many of my clients come to me hoping I can radically change them for the better for when they appear on TV. Instead, their nervousness makes them appear worse than usual.

"Just be yourself" is a common and often useless piece of advice found in most self-help manuals, but when it comes to being a good media communicator, it can be useful advice – if you amend it to "find the best example of yourself, and then ACT like yourself, even if you are nervous while appearing on TV."

The Reagan Rhetorical Legacy

Ronald Reagan was called "The Great Communicator." Was it because he was just a natural? Or because he was a trained actor?

No and no.

Although some of his background as an actor did help him as a speaker, Reagan understood that a speech isn't about the speaker; it's about the audience. He didn't speak to entertain himself; he spoke to communicate with his audience.

What does this mean, practically speaking? Reagan gave essentially the same speech all across the country from 1964, when he became a paid spokesman for General Electric, until he was elected president in 1980. Most people can't stand the idea of repeating themselves for two days, much less 16 years. But

Reagan understood that that is how you mobilize public opinion. Reagan understood human nature – specifically, that you reach human beings not just by supplying facts, but by reaching them on the personal and emotional levels. That's why he instructed his staff to never have him speak for more than two minutes without mentioning a real human being, preferably as part of a story. Reagan knew that most people comprehend the world through stories, not cold abstractions. Reagan supporters loved his stories about "Morning in America," while his detractors were outraged at his riffs on "welfare queens who drive Cadillacs," but no one ever doubted that Reagan's stories were true reflections of his core beliefs.

Reagan was the first president to have individuals, mentioned during the State of the Union Address, standup in the gallery. It was a brilliant move to personalize an important abstract message point (if he wanted to talk about selfless heroism, he's have a hero stand up next to his wife, Nancy), and it was good for the TV cameras, too.

Reagan was a serious student of rhetoric. While he appreciated classical rhetorical devices, even those used by Kennedy such as, "Ask not what your country can do for you . . . ," Reagan concluded that, in the modern television age, these could make a political leader look and sound stilted and overly formal. He was quick to edit out fancy rhetorical flourishes that his speechwriters occasionally tried to insert into White House speeches. Reagan believed that he should maintain a conversational tone in his speech and his sentence structure, anytime he was speaking. This is also why Reagan never yelled while giving a speech. He understood that in the age of microphones and camera close-ups, yelling was unnecessary and even counterproductive (a lesson that Al Gore has yet to learn).

While Reagan wasn't always perfectly smooth in unscripted press conference situations, he had a keen appreciation for the sound bite. He knew what the press wanted, he knew his message and he knew how to package one for the other.

"Mr. Gorbachev, tear down this wall!"

That highly personal, classic sound bite had action, emotion and attacks – all of the elements needed to make reporters swoon – and it worked.

Reagan understood that any presentation he gave started well before he opened his mouth. He intensely scrutinized every element of his visual presentation. If you look at old footage of Reagan during his presidency, you will be hard-pressed to ever find a shot of him speaking or walking to a lectern with his suit jacket unbuttoned, nor will you find a shot of him buttoning his jacket. These are seemingly minor points, but they play a part in creating the mystique of a presenter. Reagan understood that you don't let the audience backstage to see any aspect of the preparation – and that goes for even as mundane an act as buttoning your jacket.

As Reagan aged, he shunned the face lifts popular with most of his Hollywood colleagues. As his neck sagged and became more wrinkled, Reagan compensated by having his shirt collar slightly too large by normal standards. By never having the shirt collar tight around his neck, it took attention away from his one physical appearance of weakness.

Reagan brought an extraordinary discipline to the White House communications process. He required all major speeches to be finished one week before they were to be delivered, a discipline not followed by any of his successors. This would allow him time to personally make many edits and to practice.

Perhaps the biggest mistaken notion about Reagan as a communicator is that he was such a natural that he could just pick up a script and deliver it well on a first reading. Reagan knew that communicating well was a function of hard work. For every major speech, especially the State of the Union addresses, he would take the final text up to his private study in the personal quarters of the White House and read the words out loud for hours every night for a week prior to the presentation. Then the day before the big speech, he would spend the entire day in a formal rehearsal that included videotaping with feedback and critique from his media and communications advisors.

By the time Reagan was actually reading his speech from the teleprompter in front of the American people on national TV, he was so incredibly comfortable with the words that he could make them his own and inject them with feeling. Reagan clearly understood that the words themselves are 7 percent of the total impression a speaker leaves with an audience. The rest of the message comes from the speaker's voice, inflection, facial expression and body language. He understood he was not simply a deliverer of words.

Of course, when you are President, not every speech is as important as the State of the Union. A President must give a dozen speeches a week or more. In this case, most Presidents, or for that matter all other speakers, rely on reading notes in front of audiences.

Listening to a speech read from notes is a painful, boring experience for an audience. (Think of Gerald Ford stumbling his way through a prepared statement.) But Reagan knew all of the tricks to this communications process as well. Most speakers start with their head down and read a sentence from their speech text. Next, they stop and look up at their audience and say nothing. Then they quickly jerk their head down again and continue to read in a monotone fashion. The result is that audiences are put to sleep.

Reagan also read many of his speeches, but he used a different technique. He would glance down at the script, moving his eyes but not his head, looking for the first line of the speech. He would then wait until he was looking directly at audience members before he would say the line, but by now he had internalized it and he was able to make it sound personal. After delivering his line, he would pause to let his audience reflect upon it. While they were doing so, he would have time to glance down quickly to see what the next line in his speech was. This technique takes some practice and requires spacing your speech differently on the page, but the rewards are immense. Reagan's audiences were mesmerized, even when he was reading perfunctory remarks off note cards.

Though Reagan often used note cards, he was careful to never let his audience see them. He understood this would destroy the illusion of the great communicator. He carefully kept his note cards in his bottom-left suit-jacket pocket – never in his hands – as he walked toward a lectern. Then after he got behind the lectern, while looking up and waving to the crowd with his right hand, he would secretly take the notes out of his pocket with his left hand while nobody noticed.

Finally, Reagan's career demonstrates the power of public speaking – indeed, in the potential for ONE BIG SPEECH to make an entire career. Of course, Reagan had a certain cachet as a B-level actor in the '40s and '50s, but by the early '60s, his Hollywood career was washed up. It was the electrifying speech he made on behalf of Barry Goldwater at the 1964 Republican convention that propelled him into the California governor's race in 1966 and then to the presidency itself. While Theodore Roosevelt coined the term "bully pulpit" in describing the power of being in the Oval Office, Reagan did more to focus and harness the communications power of the presidency than any leader who served before him or after.

The Dean Scream

New York Times suggested that former Vermont Governor Howard Dean's shrieking/yelling sound bite after the 2004 Iowa caucuses set a new standard for bad sound bites, by which all future bad sound bites would be judged.

But did it kill his candidacy?

Since Dean's campaign had been hemorrhaging for weeks prior to and after the dismal third place finish in Iowa, most political observers had already concluded that the Dean campaign was headed for a quick death. This was the consensus before the yell.

After the yell?

It was no longer a hemorrhage. It had the effect of driving a stake through his heart, quickly putting the corpse in a body bag, then in a cheap coffin and then out to the cemetery in the poor part of town where poor Howard's body was buried without so much as a grave marker. The unanswerable question is this: what would have happened to Dean if he had won the Iowa caucus and then let out the yell?

The real lesson for Dean and other politicians and public figures is this: if you are talking to a group of people and there is a TV camera in the room, the most important conversation you are having is with viewers at home who are watching from their living rooms and bedrooms.

When giving a speech in a room full of people, context is everything. The night of the yowl, Dean was communicating passionately and energetically with a roomful of enthusiastic supporters. The room was small; the crowd, large; and the noise level, high. To anyone in the room listening to Dean that night, the governor sounded great. Not only did people there not think that he had blundered or sounded strange, but they also thought that this was yet another great example of his charismatic leadership. Dean simply appeared passionate and full of conviction – exactly what the crowd wanted.

So why did anyone who saw Dean on TV come away with the belief that Dean was an insane, deranged, unhinged, disturbed individual whose next home should be in a psychiatric ward instead of Pennsylvania Avenue? There were two reasons: one technical and one contextual.

Dean was using a unidirectional microphone, one that picks up sound from only one direction – in this case from his mouth. That meant that the microphone didn't pick up the sounds from the rest of the screaming, cheering, yelling crowd. Dean had to yell simply to be heard by the crowd and to hear himself. None of that was apparent when you saw a close-up of him on TV, seemingly yelling for no good reason. If Dean had only had the good fortune of using a multidirectional microphone, the sound of the crowd would have leveled out his own noises. No sound bite. No Jay Leno. No David Letterman. No Diane Sawyer.

If you see a crowd of people yelling and screaming at a football game, nothing looks or sounds odd or out of place. But if you were to edit out the entire crowd and everyone else's yelling and showed just yourself jumping up and down yelling and screaming on TV, everyone would think you had gone nuts.

Context is everything. When you are speaking to people live in a room, you have the time and ability to start slow, explain things, give detail, show a range of emotion and then build to a strong finish. Being slow and understated one minute and a little bit "hot" somewhere later in your speech can make you quite engaging as a speaker.

Unfortunately, if you are captured on television, you lose control of the context. Every sentence out of your mouth, every phrase, or, in Dean's case, every bizarre sound out of your mouth is captured and can be replayed in a vacuum. A little emotion in a speech is like nice seasoning in a good meal – necessary. But because of the context-destroying power of TV, it's as though you are forced to eat a meal that is nothing but a pound of fresh ground pepper on an empty plate – not tasty or filling, but heartburn inducing.

Pundits like to make fun of how boring and bland career politicians like Dick Gephardt are. But the reality is that you don't get to be a career politician without being cautious around TV cameras. It only takes one "hot" moment and your career is over.

You Aren't The Star Of The Universe, Even During Your Starring Moment

Many people interviewed via live satellite TV from a remote site find it to be highly stressful – often for good reason. Because it is live, you never know what is going to happen. Since the person interviewing you is at another location, you are never quite sure how the communication process will unfold, and that means you have to be prepared for anything.

Back during the Clinton impeachment process, I often served as an on-air guest analyst for many of the cable TV networks. On one particular day, MSNBC wanted me as a guest commentator. Apparently, their limos that could take me to their main studio in New Jersey were all booked, so they asked me to hop a cab to the NBC studios at Rockefeller Center in midtown Manhattan. Once there, I was quickly escorted to a small broadcast studio room that had a backdrop of a large fake newsroom photo, and this was right down the hall from a large, real newsroom with Tom Brokaw.

The technician put an earpiece on me so that I could hear the anchor in New Jersey asking me questions and so that I could follow what the other guest panelists from around the country were saying. Now my segment was ready to begin, and I received a nice introduction. The anchor said, "Mr. Walker, in light of today's revelations, where does this leave President Clinton politically?"

Just as I was about to offer what I was sure would be brilliant insights, I heard a very loud, "But it's MY TURN TO GO ON BREAK."

I tried to remain composed.

"You had a break one hour ago. I haven't eaten in five hours!"

I realized the cameraman and the technician in the 12-by-15-foot studio I was in were yelling at each other, and they didn't know that I was on national TV at the moment. Then I realized that they didn't care if I was on national TV or not. Union rules are union rules, and each believed his break time was NOW.

It's hard enough to think when you are on TV. Harder still when there is a satellite interviewer and you can't see the person asking you questions, but the hardest is when people are yelling around you so loudly that you can't hear yourself think, and the audience can't hear your distracters because they are beyond the reach of the microphone.

So what did I do?

I forced myself to display a confident and relaxed smile, and I said something like, "This was another day when the president's enemies portrayed him as unfit for office, and the president's supporters portrayed him as the victim of a right-wing smear campaign. Both were convincing to their core supporters." Of course, that wasn't very insightful, but at least viewers across the country didn't have to watch me complain about noisy workmen in the room.

I got by, barely. Then during the next commercial break, I was able to ask the workers if they would mind settling the dispute quietly outside, as long as they could keep the camera pointed in my general direction and they obliged.

The point is that you have to be prepared for anything when you do live TV. And anything can mean distractions so loud that you won't be able to think clearly. This requires you to have done your thinking before getting to the studio so that you've got something to say when things get sticky. I'm not suggesting you have such a tight, canned script that you dodge questions, but you do need to have well-thought-out messages prior to going on TV, especially to protect yourself from abnormal distractions.

Now if you'll excuse me, it's my break time now

Additional
Resources

Media Master
PresentPro™ Two Day Workshops

Become a media savvy communicator every time you speak to reporters!

You can learn to communicate the exact message you want.
Get the media to use the precise quotes and sound bites you created, plus. . .
Look comfortable and sound relaxed on TV and during your media interviews.
. . .

Would you like to advance your career, business, or cause every time you talk to the media? Never again will you fear or dread upcoming interviews. You can stop worrying that your words will be "taken out of context" or that you will be "misquoted." Most journalists receive four or more years of formal training on how to ask questions and elicit information from you. Isn't it fair that you receive at least one day of formal training before dealing with reporters? Would you get in the ring with George Foreman without first taking a few boxing lessons?

Public speaking is the number one fear most people have. And talking to the media is a type of public speaking. This fear causes us to behave in irrational and self-destructive ways.

There is no greater secret weapon in business than to know how to persuade people of your ideas and mission via the media. This is what you will learn in the **Media Master PresentPro™ Workshop**.

You will also learn how to:

- Develop A Message
- Bridge To Message Points
- Look Good On TV
- Control Your Message
- Improve Body Language
- Answer Questions
- Use TelePrompTers, Earpieces, And Microphones
- Identify Loaded Questions
- Handle Hostile Interviews
- Improve Wardrobe
- Prepare For Crisis Communications
- Use Makeup
- Deliver Repetition
- Master Satellite Interviews
- Be More Persuasive
- Get More Out Of Rehearsal
- Reduce Nervousness
- Build A Media Strategy
- Create Sound Bites
- Deal With Producers

So why do you need to come to the **Media Master PresentPro™ Workshop**? After all, you've just read Media Training A-Z and know all about dealing with the media. Right?

Well, the truth is, there's no substitute for experience and real-time feedback. In this workshop you will present in simulated media settings (so any of your mistakes won't end up on the front cover of the times) and have the opportunity to watch yourself on videotape, often second by second. With the help of your seminar leader and your other participants, you will get a precise accounting of what your strengths are, your weaknesses, and, most important, step-by-step instructions on how to solve your specific problems.

These workshops are very personal; it is NOT a seminar where hundreds of people are packed into a large convention hall. Hear what others have said about the Media Master PresentPro Workshop;

*"My name is Michael Gallant and I am the director of public relations for EMC Corporation. We were fortunate to have TJ Walker in for a day of public relations and media training and I can tell you his approach was superb. He was able to help my entire team operate more efficiently (and) maximize their message penetration to their audience. I can tell you his pace was incredible, he was extremely articulate and he got the whole group involved. We really enjoyed the day." - **Michael Gallant, EMC***

*"I put the skills learned in your seminar to excellent use. I was told by the producer that it was refreshing to work with someone who was comfortable in front of the camera and could get their message points out. So, kudos to you for training me! It was a wonderful experience." - **Roxanne Moster, UCLA***

To learn more about this workshop and others Media Training Worldwide offers, including a full list of dates, what you will receive, and more...

go to: www.mediatrainingworkshop.com

Master Speaker
PresentPro™ Talk System
Two Day Workshop

Become a powerful communicator every time you speak to any audience!

You can learn to communicate the exact message you want.
Get your audiences to take the actions you desire, plus...
Your nervousness will melt away in the process.
. . .

Never again will you hate giving a speech. You can stop worrying that you are boring your audiences or that no one will remember anything you say.

Becoming an excellent presenter is one of those things many people put off for another day—sort of like cleaning the garage or taking that cruise. Sadly, this can have a deadly affect on your career—and you might not ever be made aware of it.

THE TEST:

You may think you or your colleagues are already good speakers. Well, consider this: Anytime you speak to 10 or more people, someone will come up to you afterwards and tell you what a great speech you just gave!

Nice, but they may just want a job or to sell you something. Or, they may just feel sorry for you.

The real test of your presentation is this: will people remember what you said one week or one month later, and will they be acting upon what they learned?

There is no greater secret weapon in business than to know how to persuade people of your ideas and mission. This is what you will learn in the **Master Speaker PresentPro™ Talk System.**

Why else is it essential to become an excellent speaker? Once you learn the basics, your body and mind will get more comfortable with the whole presenting process. Your tensions associated with upcoming presentation opportunities will gradually melt away. Over time, you will learn to actually enjoy every presentation opportunity.

The Benefits
- Clients, employees, customers and prospects will REMEMBER what you say and to TAKE ACTION!
- Command professional respect
- Convey style AND substance
- Reduce the amount of time preparing for presentations
- Eliminate fears and Reduce tension
- Project leadership

You will also learn how to:
- Speak without notes
- Make PowerPoint a friend and not your worst enemy
- Use the 7 essential elements of every successful speech
- Package your key points into personal stories
- Improve body language
- Handle questions and answers
- Improve your voice quality
- Develop a long-term improvement plan

In this workshop you will present in simulated settings and have the opportunity to watch yourself on videotape, often second by second. With the help of your seminar leader and your other participants, you will get a precise account of what your strengths are, your weaknesses, and, most important, step-by-step instructions on how to solve your specific problems.

These workshops are very personal; it is not structured in a "cookie cutter" format, nor is it a seminar with hundreds of people in attendance. Hear what others have said about the **Master Speaker PresentPro Workshop**;

"I was particularly pleased with the way Media Training Worldwide customized my training session. They previewed and critiqued my videos and the trainer covered many topics never addressed for me in previous training sessions with other companies."
-Bonnie Taub-Dix, New York State Dietetic Association

"I spent two sessions with TJ, prior to beginning my book tour. The difference is amazing. I have never again used a card or notes or hidden behind a lectern. It's as if TJ freed me to engage an audience with my entire personality...telling stories, getting to key points and really making an impact. Since then, I have given dozens of speeches and am now invited frequently for keynotes."
- Mary Lou Quinlin, Author & Founder of Just Ask a Woman

To learn more about this workshop and others Media Training Worldwide offers, including a full list of dates, what you will receive, and more...

go to: www.presentationtrainingworkshop.com

Products

<u>Secret to Speaking Like Obama</u>

Barack Obama has motivated and inspired millions of supporters with his speaking skills. He has been said to have "inspiring vision, rousing rhetoric, and a charismatic presence."

But what specifically makes him a great speaker?

TJ Walker, one of the world's leading authorities on media and presentation training, reveals the secrets to how Barack Obama speaks effectively... and how you can speak the way he does, using the exact same techniques. So that you can excel at every presentation you give!

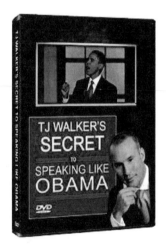

Cost: $29.95

Media Pro Kit

Whether you are a seasoned media pro or a novice preparing for your first local newspaper interview, this four DVD kit will provide some kind of value. These DVDs cover everything from proper posture to delivering messages which are irresistible for reporters to quote.

Includes the following:

Four Video Series

- **It's Showtime!** - Preparing for Your Next Television Appearance

- **What to say to the Media** - Tools for Creating the Message You Actually Want To Communicate to the Media

- **Mastering Media Q&A** - Tools for Responding to Journalists Questions while Getting Your Message Across

- **Sizzling Sound Bites** - Getting the Media to Use Your Quotes Every Time

- The Verbal Tick Buster-Card

Cost: $396.00
$295.00 - Save: $101.00!!

TJ's Makeup

All you need to look your best on TV – without the hassle and embarrassment of going to the mall or local drug store.

What is in the kit:

- Mosaic Powder Makeup & Applicator Brush (learn more)

- Liquid Foundation (learn more)

- Lip Balm (learn more)

- TJ's VoiceSave (learn more)

- Carrying Case (learn more)

www.tjstvmakeup.com

Cost: $67.00

Online Presentation School

Imagine yourself dazzling your audiences - every time you speak!

Would you like to advance your career, business or cause every single time you open your mouth? Never again will you hate giving a speech. Good presenting requires learning basic skills. TJ Walker's Presentation Training program guides you through skill-building text, video and audio to help you become a great speaker.

There is no greater secret weapon in business than to know how to persuade people of your ideas and mission. Learn how to "own" the power to get your message across.

You will make people understand you, make them remember your message, make them enjoy your presentation, and make yourself more money and produce better results - if you learn the secrets of being a master speaker.

Remember, being a great speaker is a learned skill - NOT a trait you are born with

Presentation Training with TJ Walker will help you build a solid foundation for all your presentations. Throughout the course you will develop and enhance your presentation skills to accomplish core goals every time you give a presentation:

- How to speak without using notes
- The 7 essential elements to every successful speech
- Tips on becoming more persuasive while reducing nervousness and tension
- Proven PowerPoint enhancement techniques
- Memorable examples from key speaking figures
- Strategies to handle questions and answers like a professional

www.presentationtrainingschool.com

About Media Training Worldwide

Media Training Worldwide provides more media and presentation training workshops and seminars than any other company in the world. Media Training Worldwide also publishes more than 100 media and presentation training books, DVDs, CDs and other information products and is the premier presentation/media training publisher in the world.

At Media Training Worldwide, we specialize in media, presentation, public speaking and speech training, as well as executive coaching, to enhance verbal and non-verbal communication skills for media interview, presentations, and public speaking. We provide two-day, one-day, half-day, teleseminar and showcase media and presentation training programs to fit any budget or timeframe. We will bring our video equipment and expertise directly to you, anywhere in the world. Many clients prefer to train in our New York City-Times Square based TV and Presentation training studio, which features satellite TV interview backdrops, TelePrompTers, lecterns, large TV monitors, talk show sets, PowerPoint projectors, screens, board room settings, and even virtual reality audiences! We can simulate any media or presentation situation you may encounter.

At Media Training Worldwide we specialize exclusively in media training, presentation training and public speaking training/coaching. That's all we do. We eat, think and sleep media training and presentation coaching.

The result?

We provide the highest level of service to you and guarantee that your communication skills will improve dramatically because you will be using the most innovative training and learning techniques and technologies available.

Visit Us Online
www.mediatrainingworldwide.com

Notes

Message Points

Media Training Worldwide
34 West 38th St – FRL 5
New York, NY   10018

Message Points

Media Training Worldwide
34 West 38th St – FRL 5
New York, NY   10018

Sound Bites

Media Training Worldwide
34 West 38th St – FRL 5
New York, NY   10018

Sound Bites

Media Training Worldwide
34 West 38th St – FRL 5
New York, NY   10018

More About TJ Walker

TJ Walker, founder and CEO of Media Training Worldwide is one of the principal authorities on media and presentation training in the world. With more than 20 years of media training experience, Walker has trained thousands of CEOs, authors, and experts, including leading government officials in the United States, European Prime Ministers, and African diplomats.

A leading corporate trainer, Walker has personally trained top executives at Unilever, Bank of America, Hess, Allstate Insurance, Charles Schwab, Akzo Nobel, US Trust, Dun and Bradstreet, The Hartford, EMC and has been the personal presentation / media coach to Presidents, Prime Ministers, CEOs, US Senators, Super Bowl Winners, and Nobel Peace Prize winners.

TJ Walker is a communications commentator on the Reuters Insider Network and for Forbes.com. He is a frequent news commentator who has been featured numerous times on the following networks: CNN, Headline News, ABC-TV, Fox News Channel, MSNBC, Court TV, Bloomberg TV, CBS Sunday Morning, Comedy Central's "The Daily Show," National Public Radio, ABC Radio, NBC Radio, CBS Radio, and Westwood One..

TJ Walker is also the most widely published and produced media trainer in the globe, with more than 50 books, training videos, CDs, and software programs to his credit. Walker is the author of 5 books including the #1 national bestseller "TJ Walker's Secret to Foolproof Presentations," (#1 USA Today, Wall Street Journal, BusinessWeek, and #1 Amazon bestseller).

Media Training Worldwide is known as an industry leader in the media and presentation training fields. The firm produces more media and presentation training programs, in more formats, than any other firm. In 2009 Walker set the Guinness record for the most interviews given in a 24 hour period (112 stations.)

Walker was a merit scholar at Duke University where he graduated magna cum laude. He has lectured or conducted trainings at Yale University, Columbia University and Princeton University.

TJWalker.com

News analyzed from a communication perspective.

TJWalker.com is a news site featuring communications analysis of the top stories of the day. We look at the news through the filter of how the messages are communicated and how the newsmakers are communicating.

The site is for news junkies, public affairs hounds, and people who work in or have an interest in any of the communications industries, including public relations, journalism, marketing, public affairs, corporate communications, investor relations and crisis counseling.

The point of TJWalker is to create a better understanding of communication and to learn what to do from great practitioners in the news and to learn what not to do from people who screw up in the news. (And in any given week, a newsmaker might be used as an example for both).

www.tjwalker.com

Other Books by TJ Walker

How to Give a Pretty Good Presentation

Straightforward, entertaining, and well-organized, this user-friendly resource will walk you step-by-step through the process from how to write, rehearse, and deliver a pretty good presentation that will make you appear confident, memorable, and competent. Although it does not promise the moon (or a standing ovation), this public speaking survival guide will help you! Whatever your job, if you need to give a presentation and are feeling overwhelmed by it, How to Give a Pretty Good Presentation is there for you.

TJ Walker's Secret to Foolproof Presentations

Presentation Training A-Z